I worried all the way over to the garden where we were to be married amidst a profusion of peonies and spirea that he would forget his lines. "I take thee Carol . . . ." I didn't dare to tell him what I was thinking, but what came out was more to the point: "You know what? It just occurred to me that I really don't know if I believe in monogamy. You know what I read in this sociology book? Some places, the people still live in tribes, you know, and . . ."

"Tootsie, what difference does it make? Look over there. There must be 500 people waiting for us. They all believe in monogamy. They can't all be wrong. And besides, you want to live with me, don't you? How else can we swing that?"

It was the most beautiful wedding ceremony that my Spanish teacher had ever seen. She was single and full of tears for my seventeen-year-old romance and my handsome twenty-four-year-old beau. I never got to taste the rhubarb punch. We had a thermos of it in the car but it fell over and broke up inside. It was like a bad omen for me . . . the end of innocence . . . a hot, m-- blood-stained backache of a day that I thought woul--- --- --- we drove back home and got Mardy and --- --- --- soap-stains off the too-valuable --- --- lim.

Twenty-one years and three children later my innocent husband declared before all who would listen: "I swear to God, I never abused this woman!" And Judge George Martin read his verdict on my life: "These two shall be married . . . until death do them part. Case dismissed."

Twenty-one years is long enough for me to know. The sociology book did not lie. There has to be another way.

The honeymoon came too late to make any difference. It came after we were married. And whatever tenderness and sensitivity I felt from him in those magical evenings when we first petted at the drive-in vanished before the expectant embrace of a man who had waited too long.

I don't know when I first succumbed to the image he had of me. But sometime during the first year I ceased struggling to define my place in his life and I began to endure.

Today,
I dance for hours alone in a beautiful world.
I dance with Peter, my little boy, who cannot live with me.
I dance because I never felt free to dance before.
And there is no one else who is free enough to dance with me.
There is too much love to go around . . . and not enough love to share.
And so we starve and famish and fall down weeping because Dancing alone is so difficult after a while.

Carol Andreas

CAROL ANDREAS

teaches at Merritt College
in Oakland, California

She was formerly an Assistant Professor
of Sociology at Oakland University.

SEX AND CASTE IN AMERICA

Carol Andreas

PRENTICE-HALL, INC. A SPECTRUM BOOK *Englewood Cliffs, N.J.*

10 9 8 7 6 5 4 3 2 1

PRENTICE-HALL INTERNATIONAL, INC. (*London*)
PRENTICE-HALL OF AUSTRALIA, PTY. LTD. (*Sydney*)
PRENTICE-HALL OF CANADA, LTD. (*Toronto*)
PRENTICE-HALL OF INDIA PRIVATE LIMITED (*New Delhi*)
PRENTICE-HALL OF JAPAN, INC. (*Tokyo*)

CONTENTS

3

THE WORLD OF WORK
Supply and Demand in a
Male-Dominated Society
48

4

KEEPING PEOPLE IN THEIR PLACES
St. Paul, Freud, and Madison Avenue
67

5

LAW AND MORALS
The Sins of Commission
92

6

THE STRUGGLE FOR JUSTICE
Unfinished Revolution
116

INDEX
141

SEX AND CASTE
IN AMERICA

PREFACE

For those who feel either overwhelmed or impressed by the rapid growth of the movement for the liberation of women, those who would like to know where it is coming from and where it is going, this book will offer some clarity as well as encouragement to undertake more extensive study.

My own initial impetus for writing came from teaching a college course entitled "Sex Roles in Modern Society." Not knowing where to begin with such a course, I would have been happy to have had a book of this sort to give students some sense of the dimension of the problems to which it was addressed, and to give them some sense of confidence in their own ability to survive the conflicts and pressures the course was likely to produce in them.

As time went on, I found that the students' efforts to deal with the issues raised and the studies they conducted in order to measure dimensions of sexist culture became invaluable source material for writing the book. I have given credit to those students from whose papers I have quoted or to whose work I have made specific reference, but there are many others whose contributions to my thinking cannot be so easily credited.

Several of my close associates, Barbara Polk, Lon Polk, Karen Sacks, Julien Gendell, Mary Mattis, and Jessie Glaberman, have been willing to read and criticize chapters of this book as they were being formed, and they have encouraged me to continue writing when other movement activities might otherwise have seemed more impelling. Nancy Milio made the book readable through extensive editing. In whatever ways the book is a worthy investment of our time and energy, these friends deserve to be made complicit in it. To those other friends and associates whose ideas and experiences are so much a part of this book, and whose names are far too many to inscribe here, I can only say that I hope they continue in the creation of that new society we have envisioned together.

INTRODUCTION

It may be that long ago in the history of humankind, and even today in secluded territories of our earth, where money and property are not given in exchange for work and companionship, men and women have and do exist without assuming dominance over one another or claiming special privileges on account of their sex. Such conditions are said to be characteristic of pre-agricultural societies, in which resources are not so scarce as to make exploitation necessary, nor human labor so plentiful as to make overproduction (and hence, accumulation) possible.

Today, women and men in industrial America are beginning to reclaim their rights as human beings to occupy the earth as friends and helpmates, free of the compulsion to act toward each other in a proprietary fashion or to serve each other's needs in ways prescribed by tradition. At least *some* men and women are making these claims, and trying to effectuate them in their lives.

Those who have taken up this cause are not working under the illusion that the liberation of men and women from sexism—the social limitations placed upon them because of their sex—can be accomplished individually. They are well aware that maintenance of the social order, however inhumane that order may be for most of its members, has been the primary purpose of institutionalized life. To challenge that purpose and to destroy that order are formidable tasks that cannot be taken lightly.

Is there any reason to believe that such a struggle is historically valid, that it has some chance for success that would justify its pursuance in the face of great difficulty and conflict?

What do we know about the differences between women and men that would place limitations on their ability to interact as friends and social equals, and how many of these differences can be clearly demonstrated as physiological or innate? What do we know about the material world, about the variations in culture, and about the historical realities of our time that would similarly limit our hopes for surviving such a struggle? And what do we know about the nature of human beings that would cause us to believe that new types of relationships among people can be consciously created?

Each of the chapters of this book examines the personally limiting conditions under which people live, and suggests some of the possibilities that exist for changing those conditions.

Chapter One explores the possibilities for change by noting the extreme variability of culture, both among our immediate ancestors in the animal world and among the peoples of past and present human societies. First it shows how differences and similarities that can be attributed to social class, to technological development, to "cultural survival," and to historical crises, affect stability or change in power-dependence relationships among men and women. It indicates that these social influences are partly responsible for the ways that sex differences develop in a society. And so, whatever innate differences do exist—which would ultimately affect the possibility of achieving a comradely relationship among all people—cannot be known decisively until conditions of equal opportunity are realized.

Chapter Two describes the education process in contemporary America and how it inhibits the full development of human potential by sexually based channeling, by the creation or reinforcement of social pressures, by the use of conservative texts and curriculums, and by outright discrimination in hiring, admissions, and so forth. The chapter then points out how education has, at the same time, subverted sexism by opening up new possibilities for some individuals.

Chapter Three describes the patterning of male-female relationships in the economic sphere, particularly in the paid labor market. The main idea is that the present division of labor by sex is a *caste*-like phenomenon that provides a cheap and ready source of labor and prevents the organization of marginal groups to further their common goals. The system extracts as much from workers as possible by creating anxieties and needs that can only be met through self-hate or self-denial. *Rationalizations* for sexual discrimination in the workplace are not the same as *reasons* which are based primarily on the requirements of the economy and not on the capacities or performances of men and women.

Chapter Four is concerned with defining how religious institutions, pseudo-scientific ideologies, and corporation advertising stifle and limit the behavior of men and women by producing fears and uncertainties about their worth as human beings. These anxieties are then mitigated, but not overcome, by conforming to prescribed male or female roles —especially by buying the products that service and embody these roles.

Chapter Five discusses the role of the legally constituted nuclear family in the economy and culture. The family maintains the economic structures that thrive on sexism (as well as on racism and imperialism). And it fosters a male chauvinist culture, a power-pyramid, which is hypocritical and alienating. The chapter first examines the legal mechanisms for maintaining sexist and exploitative relationships among people. Then it looks at changes in laws that have contributed to the liberation of men and women from such relationships so that prospects for bringing about societal change by political-legislative processes can be assessed.

Chapter Six summarizes the pain and progress of women's rights activity in the United States over a period of several hundred years. Historical material focuses on issues and on dynamic movements rather than on isolated campaigns or individual efforts. Special attention is given to defining the contemporary movement.

In each of these chapters, an effort has been made to achieve a certain amount of completeness and definitiveness so that anyone who desires to use the material as a reference can benefit from a treatment of each topic not dependent on information in other parts of the book.

Emphasis throughout is on the interplay between agencies of social control and agents of change. I have not hesitated to proclaim the desirability of change. But regardless of the reader's agreement with my aims, he or she will still have to cope with the content of the book as an unmasking of the ideological premises by which most of us have lived. Those who have not experienced sexist society as personally demeaning may now understand it at least as one that deprives women and men of broader and richer choices—a deprivation that can be overcome by acting on the kind of knowledge that is presented in the pages that follow.

1

SOCIALIZING BY SEX
How and Why It Happens

Whenever people move to change their social environments, the defenders of tradition rise to the occasion by proclaiming the natural or "instinctive" basis for traditional patterns. They do this by skillful use of anthropological material, or by measures of animal or human performance in the past or present which take no account of the material or cultural bases for sex differences. Although biological differences have often been associated with differences in social opportunity or social power, this does not prove that differences in social opportunity or social power between men and women are themselves innate or immutable. To reassess the whole problem of whether man-woman differences are innate or socially defined, we can examine evidence from the study of animal cultures and pre-modern human societies, and from contemporary studies in social psychology.

THE MALE AND FEMALE ANIMAL

It is possible to make a case for the *inherent* nature of particular behavior patterns among people by selecting from the world of "subhuman" primate culture certain behaviors that resemble human interaction among particular groups of people. But it is just as easy, and more scientifically honest, to look for differences between the behavior of humans and the behavior of monkeys, chimpanzees, apes, and baboons—and to point out the differences among these animal societies, even among animals of the same species who have settled in different places.

In fact, the overwhelming evidence from studying animal behavior, both through growth and development, and cross-culturally by geographical location, lends credence to the idea that the changing material conditions of life determine the behavior of living creatures.

Dominance behavior among ground-living baboons who search for food on the treeless savannahs of Africa is very different from the behavior of monkeys who spend their lives in the trees. Ground-living male baboons are large and powerful and travel on the periphery of the group to protect females and children from predators. But among tree monkeys, adult males and females tend to be more equally built, the tenor of life is relaxed, and males and females spend most of their time in mutual grooming activity.

While males dominate females in most primate groups, the reverse is true among chimpanzees and gibbons. The means of exerting dominance varies widely, and among some groups the weak combine to overthrow the strong.

Most nonhuman primates run in troupes of a fairly stable nature. Close observation of chimpanzees who resemble humans in many other ways (for instance, in their curiosity and thoughtfulness, as evidenced by their collecting of strange objects and by their staring at beautiful sunsets) reveals no signs of sexual jealousy. Permanent or temporary pairing activity seems to be nonexistent.

Female monkeys spend about half of their adult lives

pregnant, and since mating (but not playful mounting) occurs only during heat, sexual advances are a less common activity than one might otherwise suppose. Among some primates, sexual advances are made by both males and females, and mounting behavior is not necessarily heterosexual but is rather a form of playful interaction among young and old, male and female. However, in most monkey societies, the female takes the initiative in sexual contact, presenting herself to the males when she is in heat. One anthropologist noted that the dominant male in a particular monkey society invariably gets each female at her peak period, after the other males have "warmed her up."

Female monkeys and apes differ from baboons in that they more readily share the care of young, with as many as eight adults holding and fondling a newborn during its first day of life. The baboon mother will not allow another adult to touch her infant for several weeks after birth. Among all primates observed in the wild, there appears to be no "menopause" but rather a constant cycle of reproduction until death.

A series of studies of rhesus monkeys at the University of Wisconsin showed that "mothering" is necessary to normal development, and that monkeys who are deprived of regular contact with adult monkeys fail to learn to copulate as adults, for instance. But the studies also demonstrated that a large amount of playful interaction among age-mates is equally necessary for normal development.

While playfulness among peers is a common feature of life in all monkey societies, adult "mothering" is carried out differently in different groups. "Mothering" is performed by males in one group of monkeys observed in Japan, and by females of the same species living in another location. This shows more than anything else that primates, far from being determined by their genetic makeup, are the creators of culture. Sexuality is universal, gregariousness is universal, but particular behavioral expressions are extremely variable. Among humans, the emancipation of sexual behavior from hormonal control has developed to the point where sexual activity is governed more by the cerebral cortex than by the glands. Incest taboos, injunctions against marriage among close relatives, and norms of chastity among certain religious orders are cultural forms that are unknown among other primates. Unknown also among other primates is the large amount of sexual activity that occurs without resulting in fertility. Clearly humans, more than any other mammals, are creators of culture. Both the persistence and the occasional rapid restructuring of their social habits are without precedence in the animal world.

WORK AND PLAY IN PRE-MODERN SOCIETIES

Divisions of labor by sex are nowhere as carefully developed in nature as among humans. However, the variety of work patterns that have developed is so astounding that any generalization about the "instinctive" basis for such behavior is extremely dubious.

Historically, women have been engaged in work that is close to home, often building and cultivating, while men have more often engaged in hunting and trading activities. Where territorial claims assumed importance, and when the domination of one group over another created a surplus of labor that could be used to make even wider claims, men sometimes spent large amounts of time fighting or conquering in the name of those who rose to power in a given locality. Because of the inertia of human culture, or perhaps because of the advantages that it provides for certain groups, the typical roles of men and women in a society sometimes take on a bizarre quality. For instance, in one mountainous region of central Asia, women today still cultivate, build, cook, sew, care for children, and perform religious ceremonies. The men, whose role as protectors and conquerors has for decades been preempted by a national government, sit together from dawn to dusk drinking tea and inspecting the rifles that they still carry over their shoulders as a matter of pride and authority. Their skills in conversation grow even as their skill in battle atrophies, but the separation between men and women remains.[1]

The lives of women in pre-industrial societies, where the labor of children is highly valued, are often dominated by recurring pregnancies. The "biological average" number of children that a woman is capable of bearing during her life span, according to one estimate, is twenty, and in some societies women approach that average. Where a scarcity of resources places limits on the numbers of children that the available territory can sustain, women are still often expected to bear as many children as they can so that the most healthy specimens may be reared to adulthood.

Even in such societies, the cultural roles of men and women vary so widely as to make one wonder about the willingness of the more economically "advantaged" groups to limit their roles so arbitrarily to procreative functions.

In New Guinea, Mundugumor peoples expect women to exhibit essentially the same temperamental characteristics as men. Resources are abundant and cooperation in economic matters is the rule, but men and women are expected to quarrel constantly over sexual rights. Kinship patterns are extremely complex, giving more social control to women

1. These observations were made by myself while traveling in the Gilgit district of northern Pakistan.

when they bear sons and to men when their wives bear daughters. Jealousy then becomes a dominant feature of life. The marriage relationship is one of constant struggle:

> Because the girl is very often more mature than the boy, either because of the conditions of the marriage return or because she has made the first move in a bush liaison, many marriages of young people are dominated by the more aggressive, mature wife. As she ages a little, the husband becomes more conscious of his own powers, and is ready to exercise his initiative in courting younger women if possible. The aggressive wife continues upon her aggressive course, now operating through her son. It is not a society in which anyone retires willingly. Grandmothers who are newly widowed and remarried make a strong bid for their husbands' attention, counting upon the newness of their charms.[2]

Among the Tchambuli peoples of New Guinea, the personalities of men and women are expected to be complementary rather than similar, but the attributes given to each of the sexes are the opposite of what is expected in Western societies. Women are hard-working and unemotional. The community depends on their fishing activities for sustenance. Men are primarily occupied in entertaining the community with their ceremonial activities and artistic pursuits, and are engaged in constant bickering:

> For fifty quarrels among the men, there is hardly one among the women. Solid, preoccupied, powerful, with shaven unadorned heads, they sit in groups and laugh together, or occasionally stage a night dance at which, without a man present, each woman dances vigorously all by herself the dance-step that she has found to be most exciting. Here

2. Margaret Mead, *Sex and Temperament* (New York: New American Library, 1950), p. 171.

again the solidarity of women, the inessentialness of men, is demonstrated. Of this relationship the Tchambuli dwellinghouse is the symbol. It presents the curious picture of the entire center firmly occupied by well-entrenched women, while the men sit about the edges, near the door, one foot on the house-ladder, almost unwanted, on sufferance, ready to flee away to their men's houses, where they do their own cooking, gather their own firewood, and generally live a near-bachelor life in a state of mutual discomfort and suspicion.[3]

A third group of people, who occupy the mountainous areas of New Guinea, maintain themselves under difficult conditions by making no territorial claims for themselves, either as a group or as individuals. Rather, they express the feeling of belonging to the land that they farm and hunt cooperatively. Men and women are both expected to act toward other people and toward each other with gentleness and concern. Failure to do so is met with mild ostracism rather than with counter-violence. Men and women tend to perform different tasks, but are capable of assuming each other's work if necessary. Child care is a shared enterprise:

> Fathers show as little embarrassment as mothers in disposing of the very young child's excreta, and as much patience as their wives in persuading a young child to eat soup from one of the clumsy coconut spoons that are always too large for the child's mouth. The minute day-by-day care of little children, with its routine, its exasperations, its wails of misery that cannot be correctly interpreted, these are as congenial to the Arapesh men as they are to the Arapesh women. And in recognition of this care, as well as in recognition of the father's initial contribution, if one comments upon a middle-aged man as good-looking, the

3. *Ibid.*, p. 192.

people answer: "Good-looking? Ye-e-s? But you should have seen him before he bore all those children." [4]

In contrast with these societies, which differ so widely in behavior and yet are similar in race and habitat, we can find similar patterns among peoples as far removed from each other as Australia and central North America. One observer described "masculine mystiques" that more closely resemble our own cultural prescriptions:

Adulthood in central North America means warfare. Honour in it is the great goal of all men. The constantly recurring theme of the youth's coming-of-age, as also of preparation for the warpath at any age, is a magic ritual for success in war. They torture not one another, but themselves: they cut strips of skin from their arms and legs, they strike off their fingers, they drag heavy weights pinned to their chest or leg muscles. Their reward is enhanced prowess in deeds of warfare.

In Australia, on the other hand, adulthood means participation in an exclusively male cult whose fundamental trait is the exclusion of women. Any woman is put to death if she so much as hears the sound of the bull-roarer at the ceremonies, and she must never know of the rites. Puberty ceremonies are elaborate and symbolic repudiations of the bonds with the female sex; the men are symbolically made self-sufficient and the wholly responsible element of the community. To attain this end they use drastic sexual rites and bestow supernatural guaranties. [5]

Relating such diverse ways of adapting life-requirements to the particular historical and physical conditions from which they come is a job that few anthropologists have taken seriously. The anthropologists who studied the cultures de-

4. *Ibid.*, p. 42.
5. Ruth Benedict, *Patterns of Culture* (Boston: Houghton Mifflin Company, 1934, 1959), pp. 25–26.

scribed above did not attempt to explain the beginnings of the cultural patterns they observed. A number of authors have suggested that patterns emerge in response to changes in productive relations, which are, in turn, influenced by changes in technology and changes in the physical and social environments in which people live.[6] At the same time, culture patterns often survive in spite of the disappearance of the conditions that gave rise to them, just as in the example cited earlier where certain men in central Asia no longer fight battles but still carry their guns, while sipping tea as the women work all day.

Man-woman relations can be interpreted as a form of negotiation, in which people bargain with each other for the things that each is able to provide. But the bargains may not always be "fair," depending on the value given to muscular strength, to childbearing, or to productive work of various kinds. When an imbalance can be maintained through coercion, the bargaining process either stops or becomes open conflict. The former is more likely where women are subjected to great oppression, as in a pre-industrial setting— especially where they are disadvantaged physically. But in areas where women are needed for other than childbearing purposes, as in times of social crisis, they can begin to organize themselves for the purpose of resuming the bargaining process on a level different from what they have been able to do within their individual homes. The traditional "battle of the sexes" then becomes a more reasoned and collective enterprise, always with the hope that men and women will no longer struggle against each other to "beat the sys-

6. See William Ogburn and M. F. Nimkoff, *Technology and the Changing Family* (Cambridge: Houghton Mifflin Company, 1955); William Goode, *World Revolution and Family Patterns* (New York: The Free Press, 1963); Arthur Calhoun, *A Social History of the American Family*, 3 vols., Barnes and Noble, 1917–19 (reprinted, 1960).

tem" that binds them, but instead can create new social structures out of mutually recognizable needs.[7]

THE CLASS DIMENSION

Clearly, if there is any validity to the above analysis, men and women in different social classes will create their own adaptations to the environments in which they live. Social scientists have given little attention to the diversity of expectations placed on men and women among social classes. Two studies examine this problem from the viewpoint of working-class people in the United States; another already classic treatment of the subject was made by Thorsten Veblen in *The Theory of the Leisure Class. Blue Collar Marriage* and *Workingman's Wife* describe sexist oppression among working class families; Veblen describes the more subtle oppression of being placed on a "pedestal." The intolerability of both forms of oppression was dramatically expressed in the testimony of a black feminist who rose to speak at an early women's rights convention held in midwestern America in 1851:

> Dat man ober dar say dat women needs to be helped into carriages, and lifted ober ditches, and to have de best place everywhar. Nobody ever help me into carriages, or ober mud puddles, or gives me any best places, . . . and ar'nt I a woman? Look at me! Look at my arm! I have plowed, and planted, and gathered into barns, and no man could head me—and ar'nt I a woman? I could work as much as

7. My understanding of power-dependence relationships came from a study of exchange and power in international relations—a study that originally relied on the social-psychological theory and research of John Thibaut and Harold Kelley. See Carol Andreas, "America's Unstable Empire: the Politics of Aid to Pakistan and India," *Radical Sociology* (New York: Basic Books, 1970).

a man (when I could get it), and bear de lash as well . . . and ar'nt I a woman? I have borne five chileren and I seen 'em mos' all sold off into slavery, and when I cried out with a mother's grief, none but Jesus heard . . . and ar'nt I a woman? [8]

Those caught in the middle, being needed neither as a showpiece nor as a producing helpmate, may experience another severe form of oppression—voluntary or involuntary submissiveness. Middle-class wives may be able to recognize the submissive qualities expressed by one blue-collar wife:

During the weekend I cater to my husband's wishes. I watch him work on the truck and enjoy the companionship. I have to buy parts and special equipment in town during the week and then he spends the weekend cleaning and adjusting the trucks and keeping things in working order. Then, if he does anything around the house, I just follow him around. He says he doesn't want me working or cooking or washing while he's home. I guess I just don't do anything but what I know he wants me to do when he's home on the weekends.[9]

What is striking about most Americans is how far they go in declaring their behavior as men and women to be inalterably "correct," or even instinctive. One Hopi Indian who is well acquainted with the ways of white men and women, having been educated in an urban missionary school, describes his attitudes toward his wife in a matter-of-fact way. He chose to remain part of a society in which women have title to all of the accumulated wealth of the family, and in which marriages are made with great difficulty but broken readily:

8. Sojourner Truth as quoted in Toni Cade, ed., *The Black Woman* (New York: New American Library, 1970), pp. 91–92.
9. Lee Rainwater, Richard Coleman, and Hande Gerald, *Workingman's Wife* (New York: Oceana Publications, Inc., 1959), p. 80.

It was plain that I owed Irene something every day, whether we made love or not, and that there was no need for me to try to escape this obligation. It was my duty to keep plenty of food and fuel in her house, see that she was well clothed, and try to remain friendly and helpful to her relatives. I was expected to pay for a medicine man when he was needed, and was required to work hard and increase her wealth. I knew it was my duty to keep her happy. . . .

I made it a practice to tell Irene some of my dreams, whisper bits of information to her that others are not supposed to know, buy refreshments at the store . . . such as watermelons, fruit, and candy . . . and bring them home to eat. I almost always told her the news. I would wash her head in yucca suds, comb her hair for lice, and treat her scalp for sores. Generally, I excused her from intercourse when she was sick or even when she appeared too tired. Sometimes when she was restless, I sang her to sleep with my Wowochim songs. I also made it a rule to awaken her whenever she cried out in a bad dream; but I left her alone when she snored like a giant, even when I could hear the echoes in the rest of the house. And I never aroused her from a deep sleep for love-making, but waited until morning.[10]

Sun Chief's writing shows a subtle ambiguous perception of the man-woman relationship. While respecting her zone of independence, he also betrays a chauvinist attitude when he assumes a mediating role between his wife and the outside world, when he assumes sexual "rights" over her, and when he (however uneasily or ineffectually) takes on the role of her protector and provider. These are perhaps cultural meanings that come from the more recent experiences of "Americanized" Hopis rather than from the time in his-

10. Lee Simmons, ed., *Sun Chief* (New Haven: Yale University Press, 1942, 1969), p. 272.

tory when women controlled property and were free to choose a mate.

Whatever the causes of such behavior patterns, and however rapidly they may have changed, their existence clearly negates the idea that social traditions are immutable.

Why, then, are so many people convinced of the inalterableness of "human nature"? Is it possible that we are so driven by artificially induced fears that potential avenues for liberation are rejected out of fear of the unknown? If so, it would be useful to take a look at our own male and female "natures" in order to understand our behavioral propensities and fears.

DOING WHAT COMES NATURALLY

What can we say about the "real" capacities of men and women? Very little, from what we have already seen, without qualifying our observations with regard to time, place, and social conditions. Nevertheless, what has been observed about the nature of men and women over the past fifty years or so of biological, sociological, and psychological research in the United States should be of interest to us.

Differences between men and women in physical strength, which begin to be apparent at puberty, are accompanied by changes in hormonal and physiological functioning of boys and girls. To what extent these differences are magnified by cultural conditioning, we can only estimate, but in our society, most boys weigh more than girls and their bodies contain more muscular tissue and less fat.

Girls are more resistant to disease than boys. So, while males outnumber females at birth, men die an average of six years sooner than women in the United States. Girls develop more rapidly than boys and do not lose their superiority in physical coordination, verbal fluency, and social adaptability until they reach adulthood. After puberty, their intellectual superiority seems to be limited to such areas as spelling, punctuation, and word usage. While women are said to be more suited to tasks requiring fine coordination, there is no conclusive evidence for that claim.

Boys begin to excel in mathematical skills at about the same time that they catch up with girls in several of the language skills. There is some evidence for male superiority throughout childhood and adulthood in analytic reasoning, although reported differences in dependency behavior may well account for the greater ability of boys to think analytically. Evidence for this possibility comes from the knowledge that girls who excel in mathematical skills also have unusual histories of training for independence, while most girls are more likely to have been rewarded for conformity. The ability to break through a "mental set" (a tendency to respond to stimuli in habitual fashion) is required for high achievement in such fields as science and engineering. This is more difficult for girls than for boys who are more likely, according to developmental research, to have been rewarded for independence.

Among girls, the recurrence of menstrual periods, the onset of menopause, and the changes in bodily contours that are related to gestation and lactation have immense psychological or cultural meanings. These may, in turn, contribute to the way they are often experienced as either distinctly pleasant or unpleasant. The function of the man in procreation also has psychological meaning which, in turn, may affect his ability to enter the female body during intercourse. The fact that he can only do so when aroused, while women can feign arousal, may be a basis for difficulty between them.

While boys appear to be more susceptible than girls to anxiety during their early years in school, girls exhibit more anxiety later on. Anxiety is known to make easier the doing of well-learned tasks but to hinder creativity. This could then importantly affect the quality of intellectual life attained by men and women during different periods of their lives. The reasons for these differences in anxiety are, of course, not so easily measured. One observer discovered that girls who were "tomboys" achieved more academically in later life than the girls who were not. In fact, boys who, from time to time, have been seen as "sissies" and girls who, from time to time, have been seen as "tomboys" are both more likely to do well in an academic environment. In a similar way, boys who were close to their mothers and girls who were close to their fathers are higher achievers in school than the students who identify strongly with members of their own sex. Boys who are high achievers have unusually warm parents. Girls who are high achievers have unusual freedom from parental control (unusual for girls, that is!).[11] One way of interpreting such findings is to look at what happens to people when they are punished by members of the opposite sex for acting out roles characteristic of the opposite sex. What happens to little boys, for instance, whose mothers spank them for "acting like a girl"—and what happens to teen-age girls who are punished by men for trying to act as their equals? Motivation is tempered by confusion and fear about both "success" and "failure."

It is accepted that boys are more aggressive than girls. To what extent aggressive behavior is learned, however, is a subject that is only recently coming under close scrutiny.

11. Lawrence Kohlberg, "A Cognitive-developmental Analysis of Sex Differences," in Eleanor Maccoby, ed., *The Development of Sex Differences* (Stanford, Calif.: Stanford University Press, 1966), pp. 82–173.

One laboratory study showed that when children were assured that their responses were not being recorded, sex differences in aggressiveness under frustration vanished.

It is certainly not difficult to think of instances where the typical behavior patterns of boys and girls can be specifically attributed to patterns of response in the environment. A mother who remarks approvingly on the "all-boy" behavior of an otherwise feminine-appearing child when he drops a heavy rock in a mud puddle, but who, at the same time, cautions a young girl about getting herself muddy in the same puddle, should be able to understand the conditioning process that made her own girls "all-girl." [12] Parents are seldom aware of the power they have in determining such behavior.

Responses of parents and other adults to their newborn infants vary according to the sex of the child. Girls receive fondling and petting kinds of attention while boys are jostled and teased. Parents talk more to their male children, buy them more toys, spend more time with them, and allow them more freedom, even when these same parents say they believe that the education of boys and girls should be as similar as possible.

Men are usually thought to be more sexually demanding than women, although cultures vary widely in this regard, even in the United States. There is no society or subculture, however, that is not more restrictive sexually of women than of men, so it is impossible to know whether there is a physiological basis for differences in sexual interest and activity between men and women. What we do know about

12. See excerpted comments by A. S. Neill and Paul Goodman in Edwin Schur, ed., *The Family and the Sexual Revolution* (Bloomington, Ind.: Indiana University Press, 1964), pp. 169–180.

the differences between the physiological capacities of men and women indicates that women are capable of repeated orgasms over a longer period of time than men are, and that they are slower to arouse but more difficult to satiate when aroused. This kind of information is, however, likely to be culturally based, since sexual relationships that are described as mutually satisfying show much similarity between men and women in being aroused and satiated. Such reports vary depending on the level of education, social class, and other characteristics. This could suggest that there is a greater need or willingness among less educated people to prove themselves sexually by "performing" the sexual act and by emphasizing the climactic of the man as the end product of that act.

Paper and pencil tests designed to measure "masculinity" and "femininity" are not very useful for comparing cultures. Behavior that is considered feminine in one culture, such as emotionality, may be considered masculine in another. Spanish men, for example, are not only permitted, but also encouraged to express sentimentality and weakness in the presence of a lover, while men in central Europe are denied such indulgence. Tests designed to measure personal concerns about sexual identity show that such concerns are not related to the objective presence or absence of so-called "masculine" or "feminine" traits.

What we do know about the developmental histories of boys and girls in the United States is that at various stages there is increased concern over sexual identity and over the moral injunctions related to sex. Some psychologists think that these concerns are important in the overall patterns of acceptance or rejection of the self that characterize individuals in the society. Some social critics have viewed whole societies as neurotic because of the pressures and cross-pressures that members experience in their man-woman relationships.[13]

If all of this is not evidence enough for the almost infinite variations in human nature, one further group of data shatter beyond any possible doubt the notion that personality characteristics are controlled by sex-related hormonal or physiological differences. Hermaphrodite individuals, or those whose physiology is neither distinctly male nor female, are usually "assigned" a gender at birth on the basis of predominant external features. Those who later undergo surgery to change their genitalia to correspond with internal sexual features are unable to change their personalities to meet new behavioral expectations. For instance, a person who is internally female but who was born with a penis, and who has the penis removed before puberty, continues to show culturally "male" attributes and continues to think of herself as a male.[14]

The critical period for gender imprinting appears to be when a child begins to speak and to understand language. Assignment of gender is thus far more powerful in determining behavioral characteristics than any physiological features, either innate or manipulated.

Given the maleability of human beings at birth, and given the advances in science and technology that make it unnecessary for people to be preoccupied with the limitations of their bodies, it seems strange indeed that we continue to put so much emphasis on the differences between men and women and on the dangers of their free association as human beings.

13. *Ibid.*, pp. 53–61.
14. John Money, "Developmental Differentiation of Femininity and Masculinity," Seymore Farber and Roger Wilson, eds., *The Potential of Women* (New York: McGraw-Hill Book Company, 1963), p. 55.

Whatever benefits can be derived from emphasizing differences between the sexes, such emphasis does not benefit all people equally. Individuals possess various combinations of X and Y chromosomes—the chromosomes related to determination of sex. Such combinations themselves are not predictive of behavioral characteristics. Whatever peculiar temperamental tendencies one may have at birth, it seems cruel to suppress or encourage these on the basis of arbitrary sexist traditions. In every society where emphasis is placed on cultivating uniform personalities, according to sex or according to any other categorical feature, people who cannot or will not meet these expectations suffer cruel punishment, often taking the form of social isolation. Why cannot men and women work, play, laugh, and cry together, claiming neither glory nor pity for acting in whatever capacities they are able, and for meeting their common needs for love and sustenance, for procreation and pleasure?

For those who are conscious of their oppression as men and women—kept in anxiety about their worth and identity as human beings because they must "make it" as a man or a woman member of a sexist society—new possibilities for freedom exist today. Never before, nor anywhere else in the world, have conditions been more ready for ensuring the collective health and wealth of people without causing some to suffer for the advancement of others. To fear to take a stand on behalf of human freedom today is to stagnate in the midst of hopeless contradictions while others are daring to create a new and better world.

REFERENCES

ALBERT BANDURA and RICHARD WALTERS, *Social Learning and Personality Development*, New York: Holt, Rinehart & Winston, Inc., 1963.

ROBERT BRIFFAULT and BRONISLAW MALINOWSKI, *Marriage Past and Present,* Boston: Porter Sargent, Publisher, 1956.

SANFORD DORNBUSH, "Afterword," in Eleanor Maccoby, ed., *The Development of Sex Differences,* Stanford, California: Stanford University Press, 1966, pp. 204–19.

ALBERT ELLIS, *The Folklore of Sex,* New York: Grove Press, 1961.

GEOFFREY GORER, "Man has no 'killer' instinct," in Ashley Montagu, ed., *Man and Aggression,* New York: Oxford University Press. Inc., 1968.

FORD and BEACH, *Patterns of Sexual Behavior,* New York: Harper & Row, Publishers, 1951.

DAVID HAMBURG and DONALD LUNDE, "Sex Differences," in Eleanor Maccoby, ed., *The Development of Sex Differences,* op. cit., pp. 1–23.

HARRY HARLOW, "The Nature of Love," *The American Psychologist* 13, *12* (1958): 673–85.

PHYLLIS JAY, "The Female Primate," in Seymore Farber and Roger Wilson, eds. *The Potential of Women,* New York: Mc-Graw-Hill Book Company, 1963, pp. 3–12.

LAWRENCE KOHLBERG, "A Cognitive Developmental Analysis of Children's Sex Role Concepts," in Eleanor Maccoby, ed., *The Development of Sex Differences,* op. cit., pp. 82–174.

ELEANOR MACCOBY, "Women's Intellect," in Seymore Farber and Roger Wilson, eds., *The Potential of Women,* New York: McGraw-Hill Book Company, 1963, pp. 24–39.

JOHN MONEY, "Developmental Differentiation of Femininity and Masculinity Compared," Seymore Farber and Roger Wilson, eds., *The Potential of Women,* New York: McGraw-Hill Book Company, 1963, pp. 51–65.

MARSHALL D. SAHLINS, "The Origin of Society," *Scientific American,* September, 1960, pp. 76–87.

WASHBURN and DEVORE, "The Social Life of Baboons," *Scientific American,* 204, *6* (1961): 62–71.

2

EDUCATING
A NEW GENERATION:
For Whatever It's Worth

Liberal tradition assumes that educational institutions provide extensive analyses and criticism of the social order, and an atmosphere where individuals can test the limits of their abilities. In reality, however, educational institutions tend to teach a defense and maintenance of the social order and to train individuals to fit positions in that order.

There is often tension between those who want to create a more open society and those who want to close off any avenues to change. That tension is intensified whenever a group that has been powerless begins to show its determination to be subject—vital and human—rather than object—inanimate and manipulatable.

During the past decade, black Americans have challenged the educational system in ways that have forced its institutions to begin to incorporate blacks as subjects, in their staffs and in their curriculums. Today, women are making some of the same demands. But the resistance to these demands is scarcely diminished by the hard lessons of the 60s. The tendency to perpetuate sexism exists still in exaggerated fashion within the school milieu.

The following description of what happens to a young

child's image of himself or herself as a sexual creature upon entering school, and how that image is affected as he or she progresses through the educational system, will make clear the pervasiveness of sexist culture in the schools of America.

NURSERY SCHOOL

There is abundant evidence to suggest that, whatever the home situation, whether one or both parents earn money, whether both parents are in the home, children learn very early to disinguish what is "normal" and what is merely "permissible" within the culture. If they have not learned by age three that the normal state of affairs is for a child to have a father who supports the family with his work and who determines its style and standard of living, and a mother who devotes herself to serving the other needs of her husband and children, they will have these norms well impressed upon them when they first enter school. In school they will learn, if they have not done so already, that while it is appropriate for girls to whine and to stay clean and to recite well, it is just as appropriate for boys to shout and to get dirty and prefer activity to quiet pursuits.

A survey of nursery schools in one metropolitan area showed that although a few new schools are consciously encouraging boys and girls to take part in all of the play and other activities, the predominant pattern is to restrict but not forbid access to games, toys, play areas, and teachers according to what is thought appropriate for boys or girls. At certain periods, boys are invited to retire to the truck room, for instance, while girls are encouraged to take advantage of the doll corner. Boys and girls usually use separate washrooms. When the girls are called together in preparation for a group activity, they are more severely reprimanded than boys for noisy and boisterious behavior. Outdoors, boys are more often given balls and encouraged to engage in rough play together. They are given larger play areas and less concern is shown about the effect of play on their clothes. Wearing trousers or shorts, they can move about with more abandon than girls, who usually wear dresses.

The experience of being lined up separately, or grouped at separate tables for meals, must have a powerful socializing impact on young children, many of whom may have experienced far less emphasis on gender before entering nursery school. It is not uncommon for disobedient boys to be punished by being made to sit with the girls. For girls to be allowed to join the boys, however, is a special privilege. How can children avoid either hating themselves or hating each other in such a situation?

The case made here may be somewhat overdrawn, if one takes into account the innovations being made today as a result of agitation on the part of parents and educators who are part of the new movement to de-emphasize gender-appropriate behavior. But the above description is an accurate portrayal of the kind of nursery school or kindergarten experience that has been given to most children in America.

When several hundred kindergarten and primary grade boys and girls in a Detroit suburb were shown pictures of girls and boys their own age and asked to choose one of each pair whom they would like as a friend, they chose children of their own sex eighty to ninety percent of the time, with little variation by sex or age.[1] Considering the pressures that are placed upon children at this age to identify with mem-

1. Bruce Fisher, "Race and Sex Preferences Among Young School Children" (Oakland University, unpublished paper written under direction of Carol Andreas, 1969; available for examination at office of Women's Liberation Coalition, Detroit, Mich.).

bers of their own sex, it is surprising that the percentage is not even higher. Presumably there is some reward given for interaction with members of the opposite sex in house-keeping games and "chase me" activities that anticipate courtship and conquest behavior. And, as pointed out in a number of recent publications, teachers are under pressure to limit their glorification of male independence in order to foster respect for the authority of the teacher. So, some boys are bound to be confused about the conflicting expecta-tions placed upon them, and may even learn to identify with girls or with female teachers—a situation that is thought to be alarming by some educators.

An example of the absurd way the school setting makes demands upon children by sex is the experience of a young boy who had learned to ride a bicycle before entering school. He suddenly became concerned about the design of his bicycle. The crossbar, appropriate for a "boy's bike," was missing. The bicycle had been ingeniously designed to un-dergo gender-change so that with the addition of a crossbar it was made acceptable for the new social requirements placed upon it. However, its young owner experienced great difficulty mounting and dismounting his new "boy's bike," a difficulty that he was more than willing to cope with in order to avoid the ridicule of school peers.

The enormity of the anxiety and conflict engendered from socially imposed definitions of maleness and femaleness is well illustrated by the fact that an otherwise intelligent and self-confident child was incapable of interpreting the situa-tion in common sense terms (i.e., "a 'boy's bike' is a bike owned and operated by a boy"). Teachers who fail to help children overcome such pressure from their peers become part of the problem, just as they perpetuate racism when they fail to combat its specific manifestations.

The popular educational television series, "Sesame Street," has recognized some of the problems created by racism, but in building up the male while putting Susan in her place as a female, perpetuates chauvinism in other forms. For whatever reasons, the schools usually use more of their resources to socialize boys into stereotyped roles than they do to assist girls in preparing for their more limited adult roles. One measure of this is the relative amount of attention given to man versus woman roles in the reading material of schoolchildren. Some publishing companies that have gained wide control of the market in both public and parochial schools in the United States have been issuing the same reading texts for more than half a century, with only minor revisions. In these texts, with increasing frequency, men are displayed and described in "masculine" (i.e., instrumental or achieving) roles with increasing frequency from the first to the fifth grade. But there is no corresponding effort to increase the presentation of women in "feminine" (i.e., expressive) roles. In other words, it seems that a subtle effect of reading texts is to socialize boys into specific kinds of "male" roles (primarily roles characteristic of white middle class men) and to socialize women to accept the idea of a "man's world," rather than to socialize women into distinctively "female" (rich or poor) roles. By the time children are in the fifth grade, eighty to eighty-five percent of their reading material centers around "men's" activity.

By the time children reach junior high, the libraries they use offer girls few examples of female heroines other than those whose highest aspiration is to "be popular" with boys. Their school reading material is not much different from what they get by reading *Seventeen,* a magazine that includes an average of forty-three advertisements for engagement rings in each issue. Home economics courses, which are often required for girls (and from which boys are usually excluded), offer the same message, giving advice on hair styling, dress and carriage, and etiquette. Boys are trained in the shop to value manual labor as an end in itself, and to follow specific directions—skills that will be useful in a factory setting where compliance is mandatory.

TRACKING

Sexism has other effects on boys and girls, beyond equipping them each with different skills during their school years. It increases in the high school environment to the point where students (both boys and girls) who emphasize intellectually demanding subjects are accused of lack of masculinity or lack of femininity. They are given less social reward for their efforts than are those who emphasize sex-specific areas such as sports and cheerleading. In the realm of intellectual activity, it has been shown that interest and performance declines over a period of time in those areas where expertise is rewarded only in sex-specific ways. This is most apparent in the decline in mathematical interest among girls after the fifth grade.

In grade school, "tracking" by sex occurs by channeling boys into "safety patrol" activity and girls into "room helper" activity, through clothing restrictions, and through after school clubs such as "bluebirds" and "boy scouts." By the time children reach high school, the tracking is part of the curriculum, and the counselling programs are blatantly sexist. Schools sponsor "career days" in which nurses and stewardesses are invited to speak to the girls and engineers and business managers are invited to speak to the boys.

Girls stay in school longer than boys, on the average, and girls are less often apprehended for truancy, vandalism, and other antisocial activities.[2] For boys, a delinquent subculture exists which offers an alternative route to "masculine success," a route that is more glamorized in teen-age drama and literature than is the route of prostitution open to girls who want to capitalize on their "femininity." Possibly, too, where the intellectual endeavors of girls have not been thoroughly discouraged, they are more likely to stay in school because they can indulge purely intellectual and aesthetic interests, which are not in conflict with their non-specific adult roles as servants of men and children. Boys feel more impelled to get on with the business of living, to acquire a marketable skill. Disinterest in school can be taken as evidence that bureaucratized society has not provided meaningful vocational goals for its members—goals that meet their own human needs instead of the needs of others to profit from their educated labor.

KNOWLEDGE FOR WHOM?

In spite of the fact that females earn higher marks, on the average, than boys, especially in their early school years (a fact that has often been explained by their greater willingness to submit to authority, to "please the teacher"), they are not as often encouraged to continue their academic careers at the college level. In college, boys who have trained for factory work or military service have already been selected and the pressures not to appear academically competent are less intense. Girls, on the other hand, experience more such pressure as they approach marriageable age. Whether or not middle- and upper-class boys are inclined to academic pursuits, they are given a strong incentive to

2. Rose Giallombardo, ed., *Juvenile Delinquency* (New York: John Wiley and Sons, 1966), p. 50.

continue in college so that they will be prepared to assume dominant social roles upon reaching adulthood. Well-known coeducational colleges and universities, both public and private, often operate according to a quota system, in order to assure a preponderance of male admissions. Other schools have a policy of admitting only girls who have grade point averages higher than those required of male applicants. Part-time study at the college level is discouraged, and child care facilities are either expensive, inadequate or nonexistent, so that women who wish to pursue their studies after undertaking family responsibilities are effectively prevented from doing so.

At the college level, the composition of faculties reflects the hierarchy that exists in the larger society. Women compose only eight to twelve percent of the faculties of American universities—a preponderance of men are in the higher echelons, and women asume part-time assignments where innovation and a high level of expertise are not expected. Interestingly enough, these patterns are most clearly established in the social sciences, where after twenty years in academia, only forty-five percent of the women with Ph.D.s have attained full professorships. Women Ph.D.s in the biosciences have attained this rank in fifty-eight percent of the cases, and women in the arts and humanities, sixty-five percent. In contrast, after twenty years in academia, ninety percent of men with Ph.D.s are full professors.[3]

The usual criteria for advancement in academia do not apply to women, for women who teach full-time at the college level publish more than men and have more stable careers than men. They are typically, however, not included

3. See comments on L. R. Harmon study in Alice S. Rossi, "Status of Women in Graduate Departments of Sociology: 1968–1969," *The American Sociologist* (Fall, 1969).

in the friendly exchanges of information and opinion among colleagues that take place during the lunch hours or after work. This situation probably more effectively limits their power within institutions than even their small numbers indicate.[4]

Social stratification by sex varies among academic disciplines, and it is no less apparent in sociology—where stratification is itself a subject for investigation. One woman sociologist has summarized findings on the impact of sex channeling in sociology departments in the United States by pointing out that women are:

43 percent of the college seniors planning graduate work in sociology

37 percent of master's candidates in graduate school

30 percent of Ph.D. candidates in graduate school

31 percent of graduate students teaching undergraduates

27 percent of full-time lecturers and instructors

14 percent of full-time assistant professors

9 percent of full-time associate professors

4 percent of full-time professors

1 percent of chairmen of graduate sociology departments

0 percent of the forty-four full professors at the five elite departments (Berkeley, Chicago, Columbia, Harvard and Michigan).[5]

These figures clearly refute reports from investigative teams of the Department of Health, Education, and Welfare that they find "no evidence of sex bias" in several of the schools where the most blatant discrepancies exist be-

4. Rita James Simon, Shirley Merritt Clark, and Kathleen Galway, "The Woman Ph.D.: a Recent Profile," *Social Problems*, 15, 2 (Fall, 1967), pp. 221–36.

5. Alice S. Rossi, "Status of Women in Graduate Departments of Sociology," *American Sociologist* (Fall, 1969).

tween the aspirations of females and their career progression. A Columbia University study reveals two tendencies that are no doubt present in a wide range of institutions: the greater the proportion of women students, the greater the proportion of women faculty at all ranks; the higher the rank (and the better the pay), the smaller the proportion of women represented. So, relatively few women are successful in academia.

As at the elementary and high school levels, men in the colleges and universities control the administrative and tenured positions. And this is as much the case in women's colleges. In fact, women's colleges, which were, in most cases, founded with the intention of offering women an educational environment in which they could develop free of the kind of prejudice induced by sexism, have not succeeded in overcoming it. The lowest academic ratings in the nation (according to the Gourman report, published by the Continuing Education Institute for 1967–68) are those given to women's colleges.

Chatham College for Women (Pittsburgh, Pa.) boasts a course of instruction featuring

1. *Man* as a human organism
2. The universe *he* inhabits
3. *His* social relationships
4. *His* aesthetic achievements
5. *His* attempt to organize *his* experience[6] (italics mine)

Degree programs in women's colleges, now more than at the time of their founding, cater to social prejudices and include such areas as interior decorating and secretarial studies.

6. Kate Millett, Carol Goodman, et al., *Token Learning: A Study of Women's Higher Education in America* (New York: National Organization for Women [NOW], 1968), p. 13.

The women's colleges and sister-brother colleges today offer little more challenge to women than a coeducational school such as Carnegie-Mellon University, which defines its objectives for women as follows:

> In emphasizing the contribution a college education can make to marriage and motherhood, the college recognizes that through your activities in the family you make the greatest contribution and find your most enduring satisfactions. The knowledge and understanding developed in the college years are not laid aside when you enter the most demanding of careers . . . rearing children and making a happy home. To create in you an awareness of your need to develop your intellectual process for the sake of your husband and children is one of the challenging tasks of the college.[7]

In contrast, Carnegie-Mellon's men are instructed:

> Your college years should prepare you not only to earn a living in your profession, but also to be a good citizen and live a worthwhile personal life. . . . As you rise in your profession, you will have to deal more and more with people both in your job and in your community. It is important you be able to express yourself effectively whether you are convincing your boss of a new idea or preparing a plan of action to your town council. At Carnegie you will learn to apply to your dealings with people, affairs and government, the same orderly steps of clear thinking you learned in your college courses.[8]

In more relaxed prose, the Carnegie catalogue seeks to induce its favored gender to apply for admission:

> College is coffee between classes, touchdown passes, cram exams, studies, buddies, skirling pipes, campus gripes, etc.

7. *Ibid.*, p. 34.
8. *Ibid.*, p. 35

Address me as His Fabulous Frivolous Eminence, One Wise Beyond Caring. . . . I walk with pigeons and puppies and popular girls . . . I am Mystic, Magnificent! I can improvise an ode . . . raid the forbidden wings for sweetly scented underthings . . . create all manner of banners . . . keep running, we're brothers. I fly, soar, swing, bless everything . . . I am spring . . . simply because I am! I, id, sans lid, the kid, the king, poet, scientist, philosopher, Rex, winner of pillow fights, bull sessions, water battles, and all bets, wooer of beautiful women, Pied Piper pro tem, BMOC . . . Me.[9]

VOCATIONAL GUIDANCE

Given the pressures placed upon men and women students to aspire to sex-appropriate roles, and to gear their academic careers to suit these aspirations, it is not surprising to learn that students who think differently are unusually motivated. In the case of women, the desire to pursue a serious vocation outside of the home appears to be related to strong father-daughter ties—that is, identifying with and being accepted by an important male figure. The impetus to excel intellectually seems related to being encouraged by a man:

An interested male has the power to communicate to the maturing young woman that she is not damaging her femininity by developing her mind and skills. The women we studied seemed to need this reassurance. Sometimes even a subtle form of consent or disapproval from a male served as a stimulus for a young woman to advance or retreat.[10]

Considering these findings, it is especially interesting to

9. *Ibid.*, p. 35.
10. Marjory Lozoff, "College Influences on the Development of Female Undergraduates" (Stanford Institute for the Study of Human Problems, 1969).

know how such "subtle . . . consent or disapproval" is seen
by interviewers who select candidates for Woodrow Wilson
fellowship programs. These interviewers seem to take a dim
view of men professors who presume to act as catalysts in
the academic careers of women:

> Instructors, particularly young ones, tend to take a romantic
> view of female students and to encourage them in academic
> careers, whether they are so inclined or not. The student,
> reacting to her professor's interest, sometimes manages to
> convince herself that she does want a Ph.D., when she really
> desires a home and family. Often members of the selec-
> tion committee ascertain the female candidate's motivation
> towards scholarship and teaching much more accurately
> than her own professors, for they view her more objectively.
> Through questioning, they can lead a young girl to re-
> examine her own ideas and save herself from embarking
> upon a career for which she has small real desire.[11]

This process of uncovering the women student's "real
desire" is commented upon with approval by a well-known
woman sociologist who introduced the above quotation in
her discussion of *Academic Women*. Her position at the time
was no more sophisticated than that taken by "guidance
experts" whose books are used by high school counsellors.
Such "experts" reinforce discriminatory employment patterns by describing them in a matter-of-fact way and sug-
gesting that these patterns are natural for everyone.

> Determine your special abilities. Some girls do superb jobs
> in knitting sweaters, crocheting tablecloths and sewing
> blouses. Some boys change tires almost as quickly as it takes
> others to say 'superhydramatic.' These are special skills
> which may be used to good advantage vocationally.

11. Jesse Bernard, *Academic Women* (University Park, Pennsylvania:
The Pennsylvania State University Press, 1964), p. 60.

A few years of work on a job after leaving school or college, then a number of years out for the bearing and rearing of children, then back to the job until the age of retirement . . . this is the pattern upon which young women are advised to base their career plans.

Construction work has a strong natural attraction for active men. It requires physical vigor, hardihood, dexterity, and ingenuity. It is "a man's type of work." [12]

Jobs that are described as offering "special opportunities" for women, such as sewing machine operators and household domestics, are those that also offer "special opportunities" for black people, Chicanos, and other disadvantaged groups, and these are, not coincidentally, jobs that pay little and jobs in which little progress in improving working conditions has been made over the years. As long as the occupational caste system is maintained, a pool of reserve labor is always available and little can be done to organize for the benefit of workers.

Recently, salaries for private household workers have been rising and more untrained young people, especially young women, have been accepting such positions . . .

Among women, who make up almost one third of the entire semi-skilled labor force, sewing machine operation and factory assembly work offer the greatest source of employment in the manufacturing industries. Women con-

12. Leone B. Peel, "Content Analysis of High School Guidance Reference Materials in a Suburban Community" (Oakland University, unpublished paper written under direction of Carol Andreas, 1970; available for examination at office of Women's Liberation Coalition, Detroit, Mich.), pp. 7–11. Quotations are from William E. Hopke, *Encyclopedia of Careers and Vocational Guidance*, Volumes I and II (Garden City, N.Y.: Doubleday and Co., Inc., 1967); Sarah Splacer, *Your Career if You're Not Going to College* (New York: Julian Messner, 1963); and Frances Maule, *Executive Careers for Women* (New York: Harper and Row, Publishers, 1957).

stitute eighty percent of all clothing workers, and they work mainly as sewing machine operators . . .[13]

Women are especially advised that it is fine for them to view their vocational choice as a matter of expediency in relation to other goals that they are expected to value above the meaning of the work itself:

> Teaching has long been one of the most accessible means of social mobility. It often serves as a stepping stone to positions of higher status and greater reward in education or in professions. It may also provide an entree to friends, and even marriage, in groups of substantially higher educational, social, cultural, and economic levels than those of the teacher's origin. Some women view teaching as good life insurance against not finding or possible loss of a husband as well as other need or misfortune . . .
>
> The Armed Forces have interesting opportunities for women. They must be unmarried but a woman soldier often becomes a military wife before her enlistment is finished.[14]

The cautious advice often given to schoolgirls by older women who might otherwise be expected to empathize with students' vocational aspirations can be explained, in part, by their own painful recognition of the difficulty of "making it" in a man's world. The guidance texts give ample warning: "In every professional field women must have superior ability and initiative to succeed."

KNOWLEDGE FOR WHAT?

There has been very little acknowledgment, in school curricula, of the experiences of women in history. Noticeably

13. *Ibid.,* p. 8.
14. *Ibid.,* p. 8.

absent is a recognition of the long and intense struggles that women waged to attain what opportunities they now have.

One history textbook used widely in American elementary schools has no indexed item on "women." The section headed "the struggle for civil rights" does not include any mention of the struggle for women's rights. A series of pictures entitled the "rights of a citizen" bears the description:

1) *He* is protected by the several governments under which *he* lives.

2) *He* is free to think and live as *he* chooses as long as *he* behaves *himself.*

3) *He* can help govern *himself* by voting into office candidates of *his* choice.[15] (italics mine)

A series of drawings labelled "the people of our country have many different kinds of jobs" depicts four men—a lumberjack, a cowboy, a fisherman, and an electrician—and two women—one carrying eggs on a farm, and the other standing on the street (a streetwalker?).

A more advanced text used in the same school system contains 200 pictures of famous men and five pictures of famous women. There are only a few indexed entries concerning women, most of which contain one or two sentences, such as the following reference to wages . . . "Moreover, the Court gave its blessing to an act passed by the state of Washington establishing minimum pay for women and children." A section headed "women gain a more important place in American life" places emphasis on the securing of voting rights and describes women who became prominent in their times, but does not account for their prominence by refer-

15. Mary Mattis, "American History Books in the Detroit Public Schools" (Oakland University, unpublished paper written under direction of Carol Andreas, 1970; available for examination at office of Women's Liberation Coalition, Detroit, Mich.).

ence to their efforts on behalf of women. One student who
examined this text critically reported:

> "The fact is that at almost every point in American history
> something could be said about women that is different
> from what is said about men. Instead, all we see is the
> farmer's wife or the colonial women. We never see them as
> unique people who have a separate heritage. They are al-
> ways part of the men in the pictures and stories, like a
> third leg or a second head . . . frontiersman and wife,
> settler and wife, urban artisan and wife. What did 'and
> wife' do with herself all day? These are aspects of history
> that girls and boys growing up never even stop to question
> because male-dominance in written history is so pervasive.
> The teacher's manual says that it is important to talk about
> economic development. Women have had a major part in
> shaping this country's economy." [16]

In examining history books, data were also obtained on
entries about the historical contributions of black people.
These were much more numerous than those on women,
and the investigator noted that the kinds of pressures exerted
in some school systems by black people to produce textbook
changes might be helpful to women whose activities in this
area have only begun.

At the college level, the situation has not been noticeably
different. Only in the late sixties, because of the pressure of
the women's movement, are courses such as women's studies
or sex roles being offered. Even in the schools that offer these
courses, libraries lack the material necessary for serious study.
Most colleges and universities come closest to acknowledg-
ing sex discrimination in society's division of labor in courses
on family and marriage. Yet, here, the idealized form of that
distinction, the nuclear family, is usually given a positive

16. *Ibid.*, p. 17.

value. Many such courses are literally courses in adjustment to this form, and text books on "family and marriage" are less scholarly than they are justifications for the nuclear family.

At the college level, curriculums for women are so arranged that half the women graduates have majored in education, nursing, library science, or home economics. Half of all degrees granted to women are education degrees. It is true that women are being encouraged to continue their college education through special programs after dropping out to undertake domestic work in their homes. But these programs, confronting women with the need to "come out of their shells," fail to give them the information about their social structure which would enable them to understand the reasons for their own problems of dependency and anxiety. They offer little more than gentle assistance in mastering those skills already common to women, with a goal of "enrichment" rather than transformation of their work lives from auxiliary to independently productive roles.

Men who wish to return to school in later life, unless they are sponsored by the organizations that hire them, do not get even the limited kind of assistance that women do in "continuing education" programs. Their efforts toward growth and re-assessment of their lives are not rewarded in the college setting, where both students and faculty are committed to the notion that "real men" at middle age do not indulge in self-criticism or introspection about the meaning of their existence and its relation to their daily jobs. A transition from business vocations, physical sciences, or engineering to a vocational interest in the humanities or social sciences is especially difficult for men. Men who attempt such a transition are made fringe members in the university system, and few survive such pressure.

THE SYSTEM TURNS IN UPON ITSELF

In spite of the severe constraints within the education system—channeling people into well-defined sex roles that are not always or even often consonant with the fullest development of human potential—they do not always work. Exposure to new ideas, occasional experiences of intellectual insight, and the discovery of new capacities which occurs almost by accident within the school environment (as a risk entailed in the process of training people to be "useful citizens," one might say), cause some students to question societal traditions.

Movements for change, in the relationships between men and women as well as in political, economic, and social patterns, are stimulated, or at least given impetus, by people who have survived educational systems without being totally formed by them. Such people become potent forces for change when they interact with others whose grievances, though powerful, may be less readily articulated. The educational system cannot escape the subversion of its own ends by those who, for one reason or another, use whatever information and skills they can absorb from it to serve their own needs—rather than the needs of those who would attempt to buy their services for maintaining the social order.

The movement for women's rights has progressed farthest wherever women have been integrated into educational systems. This has been least so in some Arab and African societies. The subjugation of women in these areas has kept them almost entirely out of the paid labor market and there has been little reason to encourage the education of women even for mundane positions outside the home.

The discrepancies in the status of women among the nations of the world have caused some members of the United Nations to introduce resolutions on equal opportunities in education. But national governments have been slow to respond to such moves. In the United States, legislators have not ratified human rights conventions on genocide, slavery, or sexual discrimination. An American author expressed the views of many people when he declared: "Resolutions on such controversial matters may in the long run subject the United Nations to resentment and even ridicule for attempting to prescribe uniform standards on subjects where the pattern is *necessarily variegated.*" [17] (italics mine)

In those nations where the integration of women into the productive work force has become an economic necessity or a political goal, the education of women has been encouraged. Educational programs are geared to collaboration rather than competition between men and women for the use of educational facilities. Ironically, in the United States, where the idea of "educating the masses"—and women—was first conceived, progress toward the realization of these goals has not proceeded as rapidly as in countries where full employment does not threaten the smooth functioning of the economic system.

REFERENCES

INA BEASLEY, "Education Is the Key for Women"; Nicole Friderich, "Access to Education at All Levels"; and Margaret Bruce, "An Account of United Nations Action to Advance the Status of Women," all in *Annals of the American Academy of Political and Social Science,* 375 (January, 1968): 133–44, 154–63, 163–75.

RACHEL DUPLESSIS, LINDA EDWARDS, ANN HARRIS, KATE MILLETT, and HARRIET ZELLNER, "Report from the Committee on Discrimina-

17. James Frederick Green, *The United Nations and Human Rights,* Washington, D.C.: The Brookings Institution, p. 114.

tion Against Women Faculty," *The Radical Teacher,* Chicago, Illinois: New University Conference, December 30, 1969.

CAROLYN ERLICH, "Stereotypes of the Female in Recent Marriage and Family Textbooks," unpublished paper, University of Iowa, 1970.

EUGENE MACHESNEY, SUSAN QUATROCIOCCHI, MARILYN FROEBER, and JOHN PEARSON, "Sex Role Presentation in Elementary Reading Texts," Oakland University, unpublished paper, written under the direction of Carol Andreas, 1970; available for examination at office of Women's Liberation Coalition, Detroit, Mich.).

CHRISTINE PACZKOWSKI, BOB MAROTTA, and NANCY SCHMIDT, "A Short History and Observation of Day Care Centers," Oakland University, unpublished paper, written under direction of Carol Andreas, 1970; available for examination at office of Women's Liberation Coalition, Detroit, Mich.).

NANCY SCHLOSSBERG, *Vocational Guidance Quarterly,* 19, 1 (September 1970): 36–40.

PATRICIA SEXTON, *The Feminized Male,* New York: Random House, Inc., 1969.

SANDRA TANGRI, *Role Innovation in Occupational Choice Among College Women,* unpublished doctoral dissertation, University of Michigan, Department of Sociology, 1969.

3

THE WORLD OF WORK:

Supply and Demand in a
Male-Dominated Society

THE SEXUAL *CASTE* SYSTEM DEFINED

The concept of *caste* best conveys how social roles are determined by birth rather than by achievement. In a society not conditioned by *caste,* work roles would be assigned or chosen according to individual aptitudes, regardless of one's size, color, parentage, sex, or whatever other features one possesses at birth, unless these are intrinsically related to the role.

In every society, some men and women, like other occupants of *caste* positions, do manage at times to transcend or deviate from socially defined roles, or to deny them. Particular occupations may be regarded as important or not, and defined differently among various subcultures within a given society. But such exceptions do not minimize the usefulness of the term *caste* for illuminating our understanding of the social structure. In fact, the fanfare that surrounds such exceptions is evidence of how unique they really are.

Culture has sometimes been defined as that part of our lives which we take for granted. It may be precisely because we *do* take for granted the appropriateness or immutability of social differences between the sexes that we resist applying a term like *caste* to these differences. *Caste* was originally used to describe social relationships in an alien society, relationships which most of us do not see as necessary or desirable. To use it in connection with circumstances that most of us have accepted without question is, therefore, shocking and repugnant.

Behavioral scientists know that "virtually no other item of information about a person 'tells one more' (i.e., allows more statistical prediction about more aspects of behavior and personality) than the individual's sex." [1] This chapter will show, by the use of available facts, the real differences in occupational life chances based on sex in twentieth-century America. Those differences inevitably affect quality of life.

THE INCOMES OF WORKING WOMEN

Two-thirds of the population of adult women in America work only as unpaid domestics in the "housewife" role, or are, at least, unemployed in the paid labor market. Those who are employed represent about one-third of the labor force. They receive about one-fifth of the nation's income in the form of wages and salaries, and the median income of women employees, even within a given occupational grouping, is only fifty to sixty percent that of men. The median income of white women employed full time is even lower than that of black men employed full time, although the kinds of jobs available to these two groups are different. The median income of black women—two-thirds of whom work outside their homes—is lower still, despite the fact that the

1. "A General Scheme of the Curriculum" (Rochester, Michigan: Bulletin of the Office of Institutional Research, Oakland University, 1970), p. 29.

median education of both groups of women is higher than that of their male counterparts. The unemployment rate is also higher for women in both groups.[2]

Changes in the level of poverty over the past few years have left working women who are heads of families worse off than ever. While the total number of children in poverty decreased by one-fourth over a period of seven years, the number of poor children in families with a woman head increased by ten percent. In families where the head is under age 55, a woman's family is nearly six times as likely to be poor as a man's.

The problem is not so much one of women needing *more* jobs. Women need *better* jobs. According to the Department of Labor, one-fifth of the sixty-five million women aged sixteen and over live in poverty. Ten percent of the nation's families are headed only by a woman, but forty percent of the families classified as poor have women heads. Most women, married or not, work out of economic necessity; over one-third of the women of marriageable age are not married.

PARTICIPATION IN THE WORK FORCE

During World War II, working women wanted to continue to work—eighty-seven percent of those who were single, ninety-four percent of those widowed and divorced, and fifty-seven percent of the married women. Yet, when the war was over, many of these women did not continue in the paid labor force. This is partly explained by attitude surveys which show that although Americans do not object to women entering the labor force, they do object both to women

2. Jo Freeman, "The 51 Percent Minority Group: A Statistical Essay," in Robin Morgan, ed., *Sisterhood Is Powerful* (New York: Random House, 1970), pp. 37–46; Margaret Mead and Frances Kaplan, eds., *American Women* (New York: Charles Scribner's Sons, 1965), pp. 45–53.

holding positions which appear to "deprive" men of work, and to women who work while their children are young.[3] Day care centers that were opened during the war were closed down afterward for lack of funds. Women's magazines, television, and other media began to present material which made women feel guilty about pursuing work they had undertaken during the war.

Another indication of a general state of regression for women in the labor force today is that, although the percentage of employed women has increased gradually over the last fifteen years, the gap in the incomes between men and women workers has been widening at the rate of one-half percent per year. The director of the Federal Women's Bureau reports that women are relatively more disadvantaged today than they were twenty-five years ago. In 1940, they held forty-five percent of all professional and technical positions while currently they hold only thirty-seven percent. Part of this discrepancy can be accounted for by the increase in emphasis on engineering specialties, which are regarded as men's professions.

The experience of women following the passage of legislation granting them the right to vote parallels that of black Americans following the abolition of slavery. For the blacks, there was a period of Reconstruction, with rapidly expanding participation in many occupations, followed by the enactment of Jim Crow laws and other means of reversing the assimilation process. For women, there was a period of fifteen to twenty years when they increased their participation in every field. This was followed by a reaction set in motion less by new legislation than by the effect of economic depression and a psychological climate hostile to equal op-

3. National Manpower Council, *Womanpower* (New York: Columbia University Press, 1957).

portunity. In both cases, the threat of a unified underclass, rising to demand its slice of the economic pie, was met by an attempt to weaken and divide it.

Even today, some women are found in every occupation listed by the Bureau of the Census. But sex-segregation in the labor market is evidenced by the fact that women are a majority in fifteen of the twenty occupations in which more than two-thirds of employed women are found. Women are most highly represented in clerical jobs and least represented as skilled craftsmen, foremen, and unskilled laborers. Many work as semi-skilled operatives (such as packing food and operating sewing machines), or in service occupations (primarily as domestics). Eight percent are saleswomen, another eight percent are teachers or nurses, and five percent are managers, proprietors, or government officials.

Comparable figures for men show them most underrepresented in the service category and as clerical workers and salesmen, and most overrepresented as craftsmen and foremen, as professionals and managers, and as farm workers. Nonwhite women are extremely overrepresented as service workers and nonwhite men are extremely overrepresented as operatives and laborers.

EFFECTS OF LEGISLATION

Employment agencies and newspapers reinforce the system of *caste* by listing job offerings by sex. For the first time in 1968, test cases challenging this practice began to appear. Civil rights legislation passed in 1964 forbids discrimination by sex, race, or religion. The listing of "help wanted" ads in newspapers by sex (typically with "female help wanted" limited to clerical and service opportunities) seemed a likely place for women to begin working for enforcement of such legislation. In February, 1969, The New York *Times* was forced by a state injunction to combine its listings. Other suits are still in progress across the nation.

The Equal Employment Opportunities Commission (EEOC), which was created to enforce the recent civil rights laws, reports that, in the initial years of its operation, complaints of sex discrimination have outnumbered those in any other category. This is partly because local and state commissions have not been empowered to act in cases of sex discrimination (legislation does not exist at these levels, as it sometimes does with regard to race discrimination). It is ironic that the EEOC should have been expected to support the cause of non-discrimination by sex, since the insertion of the word "sex" in the civil rights legislation was regarded at the time as a joke even by the congressmen who voted for its inclusion (and as a possible way of killing the legislation by those who inserted it). Its performance has reflected this general lack of concern for the problems of women.

In spite of whatever changes have occurred in the 1960s, rigid sex segregation in the labor market is likely to end only where it is leading to a shortage of labor, or where new areas of service are opening up. Even in such cases, a job category that begins to recruit women seems to suffer a decline in "prestige," and men begin to drop from the market. This sometimes occurs at a local level only, with women "taking over" certain jobs in postoffices, or becoming "meter maids," realtors, or tellers. In rapidly growing colleges and universities, departments are warned not to overload their teaching or graduate student ranks with women because of the effect this could have on future recruits.

A reverse situation is occurring in some professional areas. Young men are being trained to take over top administrative posts in hospitals, libraries, and schools where, traditionally, women have been able to advance. In these fields, patterns seem to be forming that resemble sexually based prescriptions preventing able secretaries from becoming executives and able nurses from becoming doctors.

REASONS FOR DISCRIMINATION

Personnel managers and administrators sometimes explain their preferences for "hiring by sex" by pointing out the special "suitability" of women for certain kinds of jobs—especially those requiring dexterity and patience (in other words, those jobs that are tedious and monotonous). Occasionally they claim they would hire women for such jobs even if forced to pay higher wages. Often, jobs of this kind, such as packing fish or fruit in canneries, are also seasonal, so women are recruited temporarily. Such a "reserve labor force" is convenient for employers, and there would be no great loss in paying a premium for such labor over a short period of time.

The concept of the reserve labor force is very important in understanding how companies can use marginal groups on a last-to-be-hired and first-to-be-fired basis. This system introduces just enough competition into the labor market to keep wages generally depressed. The notion that women should not actively compete with men is used as a cover-up for the underlying need for companies to allow such competition on a temporary basis, or as a threat to men who are dissatisfied with their wages. The same kind of rationale is conveniently used to put blacks, women, and other marginal groups in segregated work sections. They are supposedly more able to stand heat, dust, and noise then are white male workers.

There are many such rationalizations for discriminatory

hiring practices. The real reasons for hiring women for some jobs and men for others are seldom cited as justification for the system. Instead, employers point to, for instance, the possibility of higher turnover and absentee rates among women. Investigation, however, does not show that women as a group are more prone than men to absenteeism or frequent turnover. Actually, a small number of people account for a high proportion of instability. The patterns of absenteeism that do emerge may be explained primarily by factors of age and job level. Young persons and less skilled workers are more prone to frequent turnover and absenteeism, and women are overrepresented in these groups. Older women, are, in fact, less prone to such characteristics than are men in their age and job categories. And professional women who work full time are more stable employees than professional men.[4]

When women drop out of the labor market, they are more likely to do so permanently, however. This is partly because unemployment compensation and seniority privileges are less available to women who move as a result of changes in their husbands' residence, or to women who work part time.

Ironically, employers who point to turnover rates as a justification for giving preference to men in certain jobs also point to high turnover among men as a justification for giving preference to women in secretarial positions. Similar inconsistencies exist in their attitudes toward women in supervisory positions. Employers fear women supervisors will not be accepted by subordinates—even when the subordinates are other women; potential women supervisors fear

4. Siv Thorall, "Employer Attitudes to Female Employees," in Edmund Dahlstrom, ed., *The Changing Roles of Men and Women* (London: Gerald Duckworth and Company Ltd., 1967), pp. 135–69; Margaret Mead and Frances Kaplan, eds., *op. cit.*, pp. 45–53.

this too. But where, traditionally, women have held supervisory roles, as in telephone companies, no such hesitation exists. Here again we have evidence of a *caste* phenomenon that continues to be justified without recognition of discrepancies. Where employers have had some experience promoting women to supervisory positions, they are less likely to express stereotyped notions about the relationship between women supervisors and their subordinates.[5]

Both workers and employers are apt to "explain away" cases where a woman has successfully penetrated the male job market by regarding her as a "super woman." They declare that she is just one of those rare sorts who could "carry it off." Thus, they mitigate the need to face the possibility that others of her *caste* may also be capable of similar feats. Because women held many technical jobs usually filled by men during World War II, greater effort was required to cope with them as a competitive threat once the men returned from the war. This was accomplished by introducing new variations of the old theme that "women's place is in the home" . . . that those who succeed in other capacities have thereby "lost their femininity." [6]

The reasons given for failure to grant equal opportunities to men and women on the job market thus range from stereotyped references to differences in physical strength, traditional notions of "propriety," and beliefs about differences in level of commitment, to such psychological phenomena as rivalry among women (who are used to competing against one another for the favor of men), and "emotional unsuit-

5. The use of female supervisors in telephone companies does not, unfortunately, indicate that working conditions and official policies in these companies are beyond reproach. The telephone companies have been the focus of bitter attacks by contemporary feminists.

6. Betty Friedan, *The Feminine Mystique* (New York: Norton, 1963), Ch. 1.

ability." To the extent that girls are reared to hold supportive, family-group roles as opposed to independent and more impersonal roles, there may be some truth to the charge of "emotional unsuitability." However, studies of older women employees who have reared families and then entered the labor market for the first time sometimes cite a certain emotional and physical "toughness" that presumably comes from the experience of child-rearing. This tends to erase whatever handicaps derive from the earlier "female" role.

EFFICIENCY AS A NARROWLY DEFINED GOAL

The question of "emotional suitability" must be considered very carefully in evaluating the justifications for the sexual caste system. It is questionable whether the personality characteristics that have been cultivated in and by men for certain jobs are necessarily "functional" for those jobs. Are the standards established by men as to level of commitment, competitiveness, aggressiveness, working hours, and so on, in fact desirable standards that a society must maintain? While they may be efficient in terms of production, they may be inefficient in terms of the total utilization of resources toward ends of human happiness and well-being. Men die earlier than women (and this difference cannot be accounted for by physiological reasons alone), and they are more prone to psychosomatic illnesses of a debilitating nature, such as heart disease and ulcers.

Men are discouraged from re-evaluating their occupational commitments once they have started in a particular field of work. They are constrained to work long and hard in pursuit of maximum material rewards and prestige. Their own interests and needs are given low priority. The law requires that they undertake to support their families regardless of the education or capabilities of their wives. Wives are not subject to such constraints. If they do pursue paid work, they are not penalized for changing their line of work or their level of commitment.

The problem has been simply summarized: "Something must be wrong in a social organization in which men may die a premature death from coronary thrombosis, as a result of overwork and worry, while their wives and widows organize themselves to protest against their own lack of opportunities to work." [7] Contrary to popular opinion, it is not primarily male executives who suffer physically and mentally from the pressures of their jobs. The health of factory workers suffers most in our society.

Whatever the differences in outlook that exist between men and women, these can hardly stand as excuses for discrimination. Take the case of women who are thought to shun responsibility. Even women who are engaged in professional careers are suspected of taking their responsibilities lightly. It is easy to show that if one is relegated systematically to supportive and subsidiary roles, one will not develop a talent for making decisions and enforcing high work standards, nor will one be rewarded for excellence in these areas. Rewards are closely tied to opportunities. Together, the two explain a great deal about work motivation and attitudes toward work.

The phenomenon of *caste* is no less expressed in the home. The basic division of labor is "wife and mother" versus "man-of-the-world." Even where women have entered the paid labor force, they have tended to consider such work a secondary vocation to that of homemaker or lover. Yet their

7. Viola Klein and Alva Myrdal, *Women's Two Roles* (London: Routledge & Kegan Paul Ltd., 1956).

male counterparts think of themselves primarily in terms of job or career, acting out husband-father-lover roles as recreational pursuits rather than as essential obligations.

These separations are alienating to both sexes. They hinder the free development of personality and the possibility of real empathy between men and women and among people of the same sex, who are forced to compete with each other. But they are useful to the owners of corporations who can take advantage of reserve labor and of people's vulnerability to commodity-consumption as a way of coping with life in a competitive society.

Elsewhere, in Eastern Europe and the U.S.S.R., for instance, readily available child-care services and open hiring policies encourage women to enter the "world of work." Opportunities for avancement exist at every level, so that nurses, for instance, can obtain free schooling to become doctors. But these practices have not changed the cultural expectation that women will perform whatever housekeeping services are needed. Men have been more willing to accept child-care duties than they were formerly, and care of the aged has been institutionalized. But in these tasks, as in cooking, shopping, and cleaning, ultimate responsibility tends to fall on the woman, and men are more likely to gain prominence in highly specialized vocations. An old saying still seems *a propos:* "Man must work from dawn 'til set of sun, but woman's work is never done."

It may strike some readers that the emphasis on job discrimination and the division of labor obscures the fact that many women in contemporary America are leading pretty soft lives and have no cause for complaint: that they are in fact parasites and are able to drive their men, so that it is hardly fair to depict them as subordinate. American women also represent the major "spending force" in a consumer society. Some have even characterized contemporary America as a "matriarchate."

While it is true that women hold large amounts of stocks, bonds, and other assets, and that they are able to make choices between one brand of cleaning powder and another, this does not mean that they have effective control of economic resources. In most cases, assets are held in the names of dependents in order to derive tax benefits. Few women occupy positions in which they determine the kinds of products for which the society's resources will be allocated. That is done by corporation executives, brokers, advertising specialists, and legislators—who are predominantly men.

It is undoubtedly true that many women are parasites. Whether they are given an incentive to be anything else is the important question to ask. It is not necessarily true that those who contribute the least are therefore the most fortunate. Many women stay at home because that is where their husbands insist that they should be, or because they have no confidence in their ability to make a contribution in the outside world. Retiring into domesticity, their demonstrable loss of intelligence is considered a small price to pay for the security and respectability they gain by accepting male hegemony.

ROLE-SPECIALIZATION BY SEX AS A FORM OF DEHUMANIZATION

It is pointless to argue over the relative amount of suffering experienced by men and women because of the occupational *caste* system. It is clear that achievement of "masculinity" as a social role assures men that they will not live as long as women. It is equally clear that losing out or faltering in the competition to become A Man subjects men to the most devastating forms of social isolation and ridicule. Not "making it" leads them to indulge in criminal activities more often than women, and to commit suicide more often, according to national statistics. Suicide rates vary greatly even within the United States, but there is always a large difference between males and females (and by race, nonwhites committing suicide more often than whites). *Attempted* suicide is reportedly more common among women, however, even where male suicide rates are highest.[8]

The male equivalent of the patronizing cliché, "women are satisfied with their lot," is never heard. Obviously, the man's role is not seen as a "lot." Whether men should be satisfied or dissatisfied with it is seldom questioned. There does not seem to be any need to justify the man's role, or to enforce it by extolling its "compensations." It is enough to grant superior power and prestige to men, and thus assure that they will neither publicly deny their role nor shrink from it.

A cynic might claim that men have been more victimized by the "pedestal," and by their presumed omnipotence, than women. By glamorizing the features of the man's role that are least satisfying, surrounding them with heroic or supervirtuous attributes, the society encourages participation in these activities. Undoubtedly, more men have been driven to their graves by the lure of immortality for acts of bravery in the service of the state than women have in quest of heavenly dispensations for service to their men. The practice of *suttee*, the sacrifice of widows on the funeral pyres of their husbands, has not been common enough to even the score.

The fact remains that there are few people of either sex

8. Jack P. Gibbs, ed., *Suicide* (New York: Harper and Row, 1968), p. 63.

who would not prefer a short and exciting life to a long and lonely one. The suffering of women is different than men's. When questioned by pollsters or interviewers, women of all ages more often say they want to be men than men say they want to be women. Women who work for pay experience conflict and frustration that must be weighed against the isolation of housewifery. Few can ever hope to achieve satisfactions that go beyond meeting the expectations and needs of others.[9]

Even in societies where women are not economically exploited, such as the Kibbutzim in Israel, and the Hutterite colonies in America, there is a general malaise reported among women. Again, they are overrepresented in service as opposed to productive occupations. Pressures to leave these societies come more often from women than from men.

To distinguish such dissatisfaction from the kind of exploitation we have been describing, it can be simply labelled *oppression*. In the United States, the lives of many housewives can best be described as oppressed.

One author concluded that the economies in Western industrial societies require that all women be *oppressed* in order that some women may be *exploited*. Women in the labor market are exploited ("superexploited," along with other marginal groups), reinforcing the basic oppression of women who are not gainfully employed. Wherever opportunities for paid employment are open to women, women do avail themselves of these jobs. The fact that many women seem to prefer the delimited atmosphere of the home, and even in many cases prefer a "bad marriage," stems at least in part from the fact that they understand that better alternatives are not open to them.

Wives of blue-collar workers are willing to grant that their

9. Edmund Dahlstrom, ed., *op. cit.*, p. 193.

husbands work hard to support the family, and are "entitled" to some "fun" after work. They seek their own pleasure in their children, but often admit, ". . . and that is the biggest disappointment of all." [10] The high point of their lives is the "catching" of a man. If one is not naturally "pretty," by the definition of the current sex-sellers, even that is a period of anxiety. Once the catch has been made, and more importantly, once the bloom of youth is gone, there is little left but the soap operas to relieve the monotony and frustration of life as a "blue-collar wife."

Middle-class wives have different frustrations than those of blue-collar wives. Their situation has been called "the problem that has no name." [11] Often unable to identify themselves with their husbands' occupational success, or lack of it, and too reticent or unprepared to find meaningful ways of relating to the world outside their homes, they seek purpose in activities which are inherently demeaning or trivial. If they succeed in those undertakings, they lose the companionship and respect of their families. If they fail, they goad their husbands and children in order to fulfill their own ambitions —or else they seek solace in drugs, alcohol, or psychotherapy.

The fact that responsibility for children is not equally shared by men and women makes it easy to blame women for failures in child socialization. If the mother works gainfully, she is assumed to be neglecting her children. If she is not employed, she may be accused of overindulging them or of pressuring them. A father who takes an active interest in his children must often do so at the expense of his career, which society regards as his most important job. He is uneasy in the role that is expected of him as a father—the final

10. Mirra Komarovsky, *Blue Collar Marriage* (New York: Random House, Inc., 1967).

11. Betty Friedan, *op. cit.*, Ch. 2.

judge and arbiter of major disputes and decisions—because it is not possible for him to maintain authority in a sphere in which he is only peripherally involved.

These are some of the problems that occur when men and women attempt to live within the boundaries of the respectable roles that society has defined for them. Within this pattern, women become notoriously jealous and spiteful toward each other, and many become embittered toward their own husbands. More than twice as many women as men claim that they wish they had chosen a different mate. Survey studies consistently reveal more complaints among married women than among married men. When women do find themselves—by choice or otherwise—outside the boundaries of the wife-mother-homemaker role, they meet with various mixtures of pity, ridicule, and scorn. Grass widows, prostitutes, spinsters—these are words that imply derision and invite exploitation.

Even young girls, whose existence is more carefree and active than that of older girls and women, are often moved to tears from being rejected and excluded by the boys whom they quickly learn to respect as their future masters. And with advancing age, the woman's perception of her role is increasingly narrowed.

There is almost no aspect of the sexual *caste* system that does not have a dehumanizing effect. Arguments in favor of specialized sex roles point to the benefits of having polarized personality types—those who are supportive and integrative versus those who are task-oriented. The combined effect of these polarized types is said to promote human ends of efficiency and harmony. It should be obvious, however, that to take the man's role really seriously is to advance oneself at the expense of others, to exploit, and to dominate. These qualities are inherently dehumanizing. To take the woman's role seriously is to obey without question, to submit, and to deny one's own needs and possibilities for growth—qualities that are also inherently dehumanizing. Occupations and situations that demand such qualities are in need of redefinition if we are to have a life-*affirming* social order.

DANGERS OF ANDROGYNY RECONSIDERED

Some would argue that an androgenous or non-sexist society would create social chaos, with men and women using their sexual powers to jockey for positions. However, such powers are now being used to jockey for *favors*, and this is even more reprehensible.

People will use whatever powers they have, or whatever powers are considered *legitimate* for use in a particular society, to manipulate situations to their own advantage. Presently, men, more often than women, are granted the use of physical force as a legitimate technique of social survival. Women are granted the use of sex as a lure and a weapon more often than men. There is no reason why either of these devices needs to be regarded as acceptable in an *androgenous* society. But even their continued use by both sexes would not be any more chaotic than what presently exists.

Surely no society can claim to be free so long as an individual's social and occupational role remains largely determined by an accident of birth. And so long as fear of failure in one's sexually defined role is an ever-present problem to men and women, both are victimized by the system—regardless of who has the preponderance of power.

REFERENCES

Bruno Bettelheim, "Does Communal Education Work? The Case of the Kibbutz," *Commentary*, February, 1962.

ROBERT BLOOD and DONALD WOLFE, *Husbands and Wives,* New York: The Free Press, 1960.

MYRON BRENTON, *The American Male,* New York: Fawcett, 1966.

URIE BRONFENBRENNER, *Two Worlds of Childhood: U.S. and U.S.S.R.,* New York: Russell Sage Foundation, 1970.

PEARL BUCK, *Of Men and Women,* New York: The John Day Company, Inc., 1942.

CAROLINE BYRD, *Born Female,* New York: David McKay Co., Inc., 1968.

MARK FIELD, *Soviet Socialized Medicine,* New York: The Free Press, 1967.

JOHN HOSTETLER and GERTRUDE ENDERS HUNTINGTON, *The Hutterites in North America,* New York: Holt, Rinehart & Winston, Inc., 1967.

DAVID MACE, "The Employed Mother in the U.S.S.R.," in Edwin Schur, ed., *The Family and the Sexual Revolution,* Bloomington, Indiana: Indiana University Press, 1964.

J. S. MILLS, *On the Subjection of Women,* 1969, reprinted by Source Book Press, New York, 1970.

SIDNEY PECK, "A Woman's Place is with her Kids," *The Rank and File Leader,* New Haven: Connecticut College and University Press, 1963, pp. 180–223.

EVELYN REED, Problems of Women's Liberation, New York: Pathfinder Press, 1967.

KAREN SACKS, "Social Bases for Sexual Equality," *Sisterhood is Powerful,* Robin Morgan, ed., New York: Random House, Inc., 1970.

MELFORD SPIRO, *Kibbutz: Venture in Utopia,* Cambridge, Massachusetts: Harvard University Press, 1956.

4

KEEPING PEOPLE IN
THEIR PLACES:
St. Paul, Freud, and Madison Avenue

A society that is arranged as a power pyramid must make sure that its members accept their statuses within its various institutions. Some of the techniques used today to "keep people in their places" come from earlier historical periods, while others are peculiar to our current stage of economic development.

Specifically studying each of the *agencies of social control* in our society reveals their attitudes about the proper behavior of men and women. Most obvious are the institutions concerned with education and with the law and its enforcement. (These are dealt with in other chapters.) Our concern here is with the less coercive institutions such as religion, mass media, and popular literature. It is no accident, of course, that these are controlled by men. But this is less important than the fact that they support the male-dominant order under which, as we have noted, men are victimized and exploited along with women.

It is unlikely that the sexual *caste* system could survive in a society that did not manufacture an unimpeachable source of authority to justify its existence. The oldest such authority is religion. Most religious institutions claim to have a "corner on God." Rituals, fetishes, and vast amounts of literature are created to make certain that God's will shall prevail. Major religions reflect the male-dominant order in their organization and scriptures, and in their histories and theologies.

RELIGION AS A SOURCE OF CONTROL

Each morning, an orthodox male Jew repeats the prayer ". . . I thank thee, Lord, that thou hast not created me a woman." The Scriptures are full of admonitions such as the following from *Sirach* 25:26 ". . . If thy wife does not obey thee at a signal and a glance, separate from her." The *Decalogue* includes a man's wife among his possessions, along with his house and land, his male and female slaves, his ox and his ass. Advice that is intended to help them accept the degradation of a subhuman status is often given to women and to slaves.

The Christian New Testament similarly reflects the antifeminism of the cultures in which it developed. One of the most frequently quoted texts in Sunday services even today is the following passage written by St. Paul: "Wives, be subject to your husbands, as to the Lord. For the husband is the head of the wife as Christ is the head of the Church, his body, and is himself its Saviour." (Ephesians 5:22–23.)

It is possible, of course, to find exceptions to the scriptural doctrine of male supremacy, notably in the attitudes that Jesus is described as having toward women. He reprimanded others for relegating women to the kitchen, for instance, and became angry at men who were eager to stone an adulterous woman by reminding them of their own shortcomings. But such passages are rare compared with the overwhelming image of female subservience that is conveyed by the Scriptures.

The story of creation, as shared by Moslem, Jewish, and Christian faiths, depicts woman as having been created to serve man in his loneliness, and created *out of him* for this purpose. She then emerges as the agent of the Devil, bringing about Man's fall from grace, and is, therefore, cursed forever. In later writings, there is a recurrent theme that faith allows a woman to *transcend* the limitations imposed by her sex—a transcendence that is not necessary for men. "Let the woman learn in silence with subjection. But I suffer not a woman to teach, not to usurp authority over the man, but to be in silence. For Adam was first formed, then Eve. And Adam was not deceived but the woman being deceived was in the transgression. Notwithstanding, she shall be saved in childbearing, if she continues in faith and charity and holiness with sobriety." (1 Timothy 2:12–15.)

Nor does the deification of Mary in Catholicism compensate for woman's degradation in the Scriptures. Mary is an impossible model for real woman (a virgin mother); she is herself glorified in her subservience to her own son, to whom she bows in obeisance.

Traditionally, women have been barred from participation in many religious ceremonies, and from full participation in the hierarchies of authority. When this could not be accomplished legally, it was often accomplished by ridicule. Samuel Johnson wrote that a woman preaching is like a dog walking on his hind legs: "It is not done well, but one is surprised to see it done at all."

In spite of the fundamental sexual biases of Western religions (and these were more blatantly anti-feminist than the pagan orders that preceded them), Western religious institutions have been relatively generous toward women, compared with those institutions that flourished in Asia, and, to some extent, in Africa.

One of the ways that Eastern religions have degraded women is by charging "uncleanness." This "uncleanness" is related to reproduction, and is represented in various religions by menstrual taboos, pregnancy taboos, and ritual defloration before marriage. An anthropologist describes the Hindu ceremonial surrounding menstruation:

When a woman is in a state of periodical uncleanness, she is isolated in some place apart, and may have no communication with anyone during the three days that her defilement is supposed to last. The first day she must look upon herself as a Pariah. The second day she must consider herself as unclean as if she had killed a Brahmin. The third day she is supposed to be in an intermediate state between the two preceding ones. The fourth day she purifies herself by ablutions, observing all the ceremonies required on these occasions. Until then she must neither bathe nor wash any part of her body, nor shed tears. She must be very careful not to kill any insect, or any other living creature. She must not ride on a horse, an elephant or a bullock, nor travel in a palanquin, a dooly or a carriage. She must not anoint her head with oil, or play at dice or other games or use sandalwood, musk, or perfumes of any kind. She must not lie on a bed or sleep during the day. She must not brush her teeth or rinse out her mouth. The mere wish to cohabit with her husband would be a serious sin. She must not think of the gods or of the sun, or of the sacrifices and worship due to them. She is forbidden to salute persons of high rank. If several women in this unclean state should find themselves together in one place they must not speak to or touch each other. A woman in this condition must not go near her children, touch them or play with them. After living thus in retirement for three days, on the fourth day she must take off the garments that she has been wearing, and these must be immediately given to the washerman. She must then put on a clean cloth and another over it, and go to the river to purify herself by bathing. On her way there she must walk with her head bent, and must take the greatest care to glance at nobody, for her looks would defile any person on whom they rested. When she has reached the river she must first enter the water and fill the copper vessel, or chamber, which she has brought with her from the house. Then, returning to the bank, she must thoroughly cleanse her teeth, rinse out her mouth twelve times and wash her hands and feet. She must then enter the water and plunge twelve times into it, immersing the whole of her body. She must take the greatest care while doing this not to look at any living soul, and to this end each time her head rises above the water she must turn her eyes towards the sun. On coming out of the water she must take a little fresh cowdung, some *tulasi* and some earth; these she must mix together in a little water, until they make a thin paste, and with this she must thoroughly rub her hands and feet and then her whole body. After this she must re-enter the water, and completely immerse herself twenty-four times. When she again leaves the water she must rub herself over with saffron, and again dip three times in the water. Then mixing saffron in a little water, she must drink some and pour the rest on her head, after which she must put on a pure cloth freshly washed and the little bodice called *ravikai*. She may then paint the little round red mark on her forehead called *kunkuma* and return home. On entering the house she must take special care that her eyes do not rest on her children, for they would thereby be exposed to the greatest danger. She must immediately send for a Brahmin *purohita* so that he may complete her purification. On his arrival this venerable person first plaits together thirty-two stalks of *darbha* grass, to make the ring called *pavitram*, which he dips in consecrated water that he has brought with him. The woman then takes another bath, drinks a little of the consecrated water, places the *pavitram* on the ring finger of the right hand, and drinks some *panchagavia* or some cow's milk. After these ceremonies her purification is complete.[1]

For a man to have sexual relations with a woman in an "unclean" state is thought to produce debility in him. Such beliefs are given as the basis for the strict segregation of the sexes in cultures dominated by Moslem or Confucian religions. The custom of *purdah*, which keeps women in seclusion or behind the veil, is widely practiced in some of the most populous regions in the world, thus subjecting millions of women to a jaded existence in tiny, dark, airless rooms, often isolated from contact even with other women.

Although the practice of *purdah* is largely confined to Moslem families, and is now being challenged within some of these, there are practices in nearly all cultures that accomplish the same purpose of immobilizing or hobbling women. Where this hobbling is dictated by religious practices, it is done ostensibly to limit sexual encounters. Conformity is ensured by granting superior prestige to willing adherents. Women who displayed the tiniest feet in pre-revolutionary China were honored, although this could only be accomplished by extreme suffering. An anthropologist observed women in Palestine who had their ankles connected together by chains to which bells were attached, Arabian women who walked on heavy stilts or pedestals that effectively crippled them, and Nigerian women who wore brass rods weighing about fifteen pounds coiled around their legs.

The religious grounds for such hobbling devices are less important in Western cultures, but hobbling has been similarly honored by such customs as hooped skirts, bustles, corsets, and high-heeled shoes.

1. Abbe J. A. Dubois, *Hindu Manners, Customs and Ceremonies*, 2 Vols. (Oxford: Clarendon Press, 1897), pp. 713–14.

The contemporary furor over the wearing of slacks to school by American girls may be interpreted as evidence of rebellion against sexism. Likewise, the battle over the right of schoolboys to wear long hair. For the first time in the United States, the dictates of custom in sex-typing dress are being legally challenged as an infringement on basic human rights.[2] Here, the "shamefulness" of sexuality is being challenged by young people who speak and act with less restraint regarding sexual matters.

Looking at the "roots of culture" often reveals subtle connections between thought and action. Justification for sexist customs are clearly seen in ancient religious laws, such as the Hindu Law of Manu:

> Day and night must women be held by their protectors in a state of dependence. Their fathers protect them in childhood; their husbands protect them in youth; their sons protect them in age: a woman is never fit for independence . . . No man, indeed, can wholly restrain women by violent measures; but by these expedients they may be restrained. Let the husband keep his wife employed in the collection and expenditure of wealth, in purification and female duty, in the preparation of daily food, and the superintendence of household utensils. By confinement at home, even under affectionate and observant guardians, they are not secure; but those women are truly secure, who are guarded by their own good inclinations.[3]

A Confucian marriage manual includes the following ad-

2. At least half a dozen states have declared hair codes in schools unconstitutional; however, the United States Supreme Court, so far, has not acted to support these decisions, and in fact included in a case supporting the right of students to wear arm bands as a symbol of political protest a disclaimer regarding the applicability of this decision to the question of dress codes and hair style regulations.

3. David Mace and Vera Mace, *Marriage East and West* (New York: Doubleday & Company, Inc., 1959, 1960), p. 70.

monitions: "The five worst infirmities that afflict the female are indocility, discontent, slander, jealousy, and silliness . . . Such is the stupidity of her character, that it is incumbent upon her, in every particular, to distrust herself and to obey her husband." Ostensibly for their own protection, women are guarded from knowledge and access to the world beyond their own doorsteps. "Educate a woman and you put a knife into the hands of a monkey." [4]

In such isolation, ignorance, and dependence, little is gained by nonconformity. Women are further prevented from rebelling against their "lords and masters" by religious injunctions that promise them suffering in the next world for failure to live up to their role expectations. One of the most telling of the threats used to keep women in line is the threat of being expelled from living in the same house with one's husband in the afterlife. The ignominy of such a life, either in the present or the future, is something to be feared more than the terror and/or confinement of living with a cruel master. The situation is not much different now in an industrialized society, such as the United States, when marital conflict resulting in divorce takes more than twice as long, on the average, if the wife initiates the idea of separation than if the husband does. For most women, the need for association with a man takes precedence over whatever other interests or plans they may have.

Religious doctrines and exhortations have, in sanctifying the family and the patriarchal order, given either overt or covert encouragement to a number of practices that are part of the double standard of sexual morality. Among these are adultery (for men only, but not with another's wife), prostitution (for females only), infanticide (for women only, and allegedly practiced only in hard times), *suttee* (widow-

4. *Ibid.*, pp. 74, 78.

burning—said to have originated in the desire to control poisoning of husbands by wives), child marriage (brides being consistently younger than grooms), polygamy (in all cases associated with major religions, meaning several or many wives or concubines, not several or many husbands), arranged marriages (with veto power granted exclusively to men), illegitimacy (with children defined as the property of men or else altogether lacking in status), wife-selling, wife-beating, slavery through marriage (divorce being sanctioned only for men), and prohibitions regarding birth control and abortion.

Sometimes the Scriptures express only subtle acceptance of these practices by setting limits beyond which they are said to be abusive. Precise directions are given in order to encourage "moderation." For instance, the practice of concubinage was carefully regulated in China from the time of Confucius. The wife was entitled to have dominion over all concubines—and, in return for this privilege, she was to display no jealousy. Jealousy on the part of wives was a recognized ground for divorce.

An example of one of the more subtle ways in which religious institutions justify moral double standards is the Eastern Orthodox Church's differentiation between the bride and bridegroom during the marriage ceremony. The bride is taken aside for a special incantation, reinforced by the sprinkling of holy water on her head. Here, she is made to understand the submissive qualities of a good wife, and the primary function of herself as the bearer of her husband's sons (not daughters). No such special ceremonial is needed, evidently, to ensure that the groom will perform his part well. As in Christian marriages, generally, the link is made between "man and wife," rather than between "man and woman" or "husband and wife."

In the holy Scriptures, specific instructions about how to treat women are given to men—what methods of chastisement to use when necessary, what demands to place on her eating behavior, how to speak to her in the company of strangers and guests, and how to keep her from wandering. The substance of all this is quite simple: in order to reap the benefits of the patriarchal order, one must adhere to it rigidly. One must resist temptations to treat women as friends or equals—or suffer dire consequences.

Since the rigid hierarchy of patriarchal society demands that everyone exploit someone else, the proper lines of authority are outlined in scriptures and endorsed in rituals. Men are expected to master the language and behavior of the appropriate dominance roles. Within this system, men are usually indoctrinated in ethnocentrism and unquestioning obedience. In the case of the Islamic, Jewish, and Christian religions, especially, this is apparent in the concept of the Holy War. Man is expected to glorify and take pleasure in the suffering and death of his opponents, and to place his trust in the absolute authority of God.

> Allah well knows those of you who prevent others from following the Apostle; who say to their comrades: "Join our side," and seldom take part in the fighting, being ever reluctant to assist you. When fear overtakes them they look to you for help, their eyes rolling as though they were on the point of death. But once they are out of danger they assail you with their sharp tongues, covetously demanding the richest part of the booty. Such men have no faith. Allah will bring their deeds to nothing. That is no difficult thing for Allah. (*Holy Koran.*)

> All the wicked of the earth thou dost count as dross; therefore I love thy testimonies. My flesh trembles for fear of

thee, and I am afraid of thy judgments. (*Psalm* 119:119, 120.)

Most of the Scriptures are conversations between men, the subject and object both being understood as masculine, not neuter. For instance, "Creator of the heavens and the earth, He has given you wives from among yourselves to multiply you, and cattle male and female. Nothing can be compared with Him. He alone hears all and sees all." (*Holy Koran.*) A great deal of advice is given to help men achieve self-discipline so that they will not be vulnerable to temptresses.

Women presumably find comfort in religion because it sanctifies their oppression and provides them with an emotional release and a kind of masochistic pleasure, which is better than nothing. One of the ironies of history is that those who are oppressed often cooperate enthusiastically in perpetuating the system of oppression. It seems to be a way of convincing oneself that one's own suffering within a coercive system is not "in vain." It is necessary to ensure that the system continue to be legitimized; otherwise, one would suffer either certain punishment or loss of face for one's own gullibility.

THE EFFECTS OF POPULAR PSYCHOLOGY

Where religion has waned as a source of authority in the social lives of human beings, "scientific" theologies have appeared to take its place. Most important have been the Freudian and neo-Freudian doctrines with their insistence on the notion that "anatomy is destiny" for women. This notion has been used in every academic discipline as well as in novels, poetry, plays, and popular literature, to convince women that they can be personally fulfilled only through romantic identification with a man and the procreation and rearing of his children. All other pursuits are abnormal, a reflection of "neurosis" or "sublimation." In Freudian psychology, femaleness is thought of as a "deficiency" for which the ability to rear children is a compensation. A female tendency to masochism during sexual relations is interpreted as another "compensatory device," rather than as an extension of sex-role expectations that are culturally derived. Such tendencies, however, are not found in all cultures.

The Freudian definition is most prevalent in the United States. It is most effective in perpetuating the *caste* system when it becomes a part of the popular literature. Each season, variations of the *Life With Women, and How to Survive It* are published. A male doctor humorizes in prose about the destiny of a newborn girl:

> All her actions for the next fifty years are governed by those two tiny glands within her abdomen called ovaries, for therein lies the future of the human race. So why should she bother with such things as bridges, buildings, manufacturing, interpreting the scriptures, making laws for the conduct of mankind, or the secrets of the stars? . . . She will enjoy the products of man's inventive genius and inquiring mind, and respect the laws he has laid down for the conduct of the race (at least in principle), but she will feel no twinges of conscience should occasion arise when disregard of them seems to be for the benefit of herself and her young . . . She has a quick and receptive brain and can compete with men on most any educational level but everything she learns blots out some of her feminine instinct . . . Her reasoning powers are purely a handicap in any crisis and are quickly discarded so her intuition may take over . . . She is largely insensible to pain, and, more astonishing, seems to enjoy the sensation. . . . She is strictly an individualist at heart and cares nothing about the rest

of the world outside her own little family. I know this will bring screams of protest; there are women who seem to be great humanitarians, but they are the exception and are such because their lives are so dull they cannot stand them, or else they are women who have been thwarted in their natural functions . . .[5]

The same author advises men:

You may be growing more like a machine every day, but try to develop yourself so that you will remain a ballbearing mechanism and not a simple abacus. The time will come when she demands the right to step out and become a personality, but if she is worth having she will soon tire of that and reassume her proper role . . . If she is a gentle little homebody who thinks ninety-nine cents is so much cheaper than a dollar, get down on your knees at night and thank God for the many blessings bestowed upon you . . . You can live most happily with her for a lifetime if you will always remember that she is a different sort of an animal, created specially for a certain purpose, and that the easy companionship that may exist between males is forever impossible between you two.[6]

Wherever such advice is allowed to flourish, cultural barriers are created between men and women that can make their lives together almost unbearable. Manipulation replaces communication, and humor serves to mitigate the sense of frustration experienced by manipulated and manipulator alike. The cartoons that appear in the daily papers are evidence of the kind of "putting down" that is generated by the sexual *caste* system. A man is shown consoling his overburdened wife: "But you must remember that 'never-ending

5. Joseph Peck, *Life With Women and How to Survive It* (Englewood Cliffs, N.J.: Prentice-Hall, Inc., 1961), pp. 4–5.
6. *Ibid.,* p. 137.

work' is necessary for housewives . . . it keeps them from running in packs through department stores and destroying things." Another husband explains his domestic role: "I have the final say around here . . . but let's put it this way . . . I'm the captain and Mama is the mate. I steer the ship and she takes care of all the small things." Wife: "How come you never voice an opinion?" Husband: "Well, Sweetie, it's just that there are rarely any decisions worthy of my consideration!" [7]

A woman English professor has complained that reviewers of novels, plays, and poetry never fail to allude to the sex of the writer and its supposed effects on the product. A noted male novelist claims that he writes with his testicles, and a modern Dr. Johnson, hoping to insult a rival, says that "he reminds me of nothing so much as a woman writer."

It is one thing to insist upon being evaluated on the basis of merit rather than on the basis of sex, but it is another to fail to recognize that the "two cultures" represented by the sexual caste system lead to different perspectives on life, as revealed in literature. The cavalier appraisal of the sexual act, as expressed in the writings of Henry Miller or Norman Mailer, for instance, is in sharp contrast with the self-doubt and unfulfilled yearnings expressed by a Doris Lessing . . . not to mention the vendettas coming from the contemporary women's liberation movements, such as S.C.U.M. (Society for Cutting Up Men), *Manifesto*, and I B.I.T.C.H.[8]

The writings of men and women are not always simply "reflections" of a culture. They may be attempts to cope with,

7. Carl Grubert, "Freckles and His Friends" (Field Enterprises, 1969); and B. Barnes, "The Better Half" (Register and Tribune Syndicates, 1969).
8. Valerie Solanes, *Scum Manifesto;* and Caroline Hennessey, *I B.I.T.C.H.* (New York: Lancer Books, 1970).

as well as to manipulate social structure and character development—and it is not always easy to tell the difference. In an evidently well-intentioned attempt to teach old marrieds *The Art of Loving,* the author says:

> There is masculinity and femininity in *character* as well as in sexual *function.* The masculine character can be defined as having the qualities of penetration, guidance, activity, discipline and adventurousness; the feminine character by the qualities of productive receptiveness, protection, realism, endurance, motherliness . . . Mother is the home we come from, she is nature, soil, the ocean; father does not represent any such natural home. He has little connection with the child in the first years of its life, and his importance for the child in this early period cannot be compared with that of mother. But while father does not represent the natural world, he represents the other pole of human existence; the world of thought, of man-made things, of law and order, of discipline, of travel and adventure. Father is the one who teaches the child, who shows him the road into the world.[9]

The sexual division of labor is accentuated by tying it, through analogy, to certain supposedly biological and immutable characteristics. Conflict can presumably be avoided by justifying the hierarchial order within the family as a "natural" thing—and thus, in effect, perpetuating or intensifying it. To a certain extent, the use of such analogies may be a product of ignorance or fear that comes from the kind of literalistic explanation of natural events and functions common among ancient peoples, but such misunderstandings cannot account for the widespread use of naturalistic explanations among educated people today.

9. Erich Fromm, *The Art of Loving* (New York: Harper & Row, Publishers, 1956), pp. 36, 42.

A popular child-guidance expert advises women and men to cheerfully succumb to their own degradation as human beings, for the sake of family stability:

> Life is easier when most men and women are not engaged in mutual competition and rivalry . . . In some (happy) families, children will get the message that a male's destiny is to make a mark in the world and to leave traces in time and eternity . . . Such a view is successful if men and women accept their different roles with satisfaction, show appreciation for each other's position and share interest in each other's achievements . . . Still a different message comes from a home where the sexual roles are reversed. The woman is boss in word and deed. The man in such a home seems to avoid being the head of the house . . . In such homes, children grow up with little respect or admiration of men.

He concludes:

> Since the majority of girls are destined to be wives and mothers, their public and private expectations should enable them to derive deep satisfaction from these roles.[10]

The description of role reversal as something to be avoided is one more indication of the need to control behavior through indoctrination. The quoted sections above, which are multiplied many times over in the writings of educators, psychologists, psychiatrists, and other "experts," is a modern counterpart to the religious pedantry which characterized earlier eras, and which still exists in many ethnic groups.

10. Haim Ginott, *Between Parent and Child* (New York: Macmillan Co., 1965), pp. 167–77.

ADVICE AND CONSENT

Essentially, the same purposes are served by newspaper columnists whose daily advice on sex-role behavior is read by millions. The guiding principles evident in the writings of Ann Landers and Abigail van Buren, for example, indicate prevailing values.

In these columns, wives are exhorted to deal sympathetically with wayward husbands and to demand no special favors or romantic attentions. Husbands are encouraged to expect special favors and romantic attentions from wives. Girls are told to respect the wishes of their boyfriends or husbands when they disagree over dress, over hobbies or other interests, over whether or not to adopt children, and over any one of a number of activities or habits that affect their lives. These columnists suggest, in fact, that girls should submit to the wishes of men not just for the sake of peace, but for their own good, intimating that they should not trust their own judgments.

The columnists declare that boys should be expected to manage their own sexual lives without parental interference, and that wives should not unduly resent the premarital or extramarital sexual relations of their mates. Ann Landers explains the double standard: "When a fellow asks The Big Question, it doesn't necessarily mean he is not the hero you have been waiting for. Even heroes ask. If the girl says yes, however, he may well decide she is not the heroine HE has been waiting for." [11] It follows that parents should protect

11. This quotation was selected from a sampling made by myself of the daily columns written by Ann Landers and Abigail van Buren in the fall and winter of 1968 and 1969. It appeared in the *Detroit Free Press* (October 10, 1968).

their unmarried daughters from sexual exploitation, and married women should remain faithful to their husbands at all cost. In fact, they should blame themselves if either they or their husbands are sexually dissatisfied. And they should count their blessings rather than complain about their husbands' faults, or pine for old lovers.

According to these same "experts," children whose fathers don't drink *and whose mothers don't work* should be supremely grateful and happy. They also suggest that parents who do not conform to stereotyped sex roles may produce sexual aberrations in their children.

The fear of abnormality has been combined with pseudo-scientific analysis to create the impression that the existence of homosexuality is evidence of a need for greater emphasis on the differences between the sexes. Even learned treatises fail to point out that when homosexuality is rooted in anxiety it results from *too great* a cultural emphasis on sexual differences. The writings of psychiatrists are full of references to the need for building "self-identity" through inculcation of exclusively "masculine" and "feminine" qualities. It doesn't seem to occur to readers that striving for such narrowly defined identities serves the needs of profiteers, including psychiatrists, better than it serves their own.

ACADÉME

In any "behavioral science," even if systematic observation is the basis for research, the distinction between what "is" and what "might be" is seldom made. Thus, a description of role behavior often appears as a justification or defense of such behavior. Where systematic observations are not made, sociologists rarely make any distinction between what is "reasonable" (i.e., culturally accepted) and what is either right or true. Some sociologists claim that in all societies men assume innovative task-oriented roles and women assume integrative socio-emotional roles (simply discounting contrary evidence as unbelievable). Therefore, they conclude, this must be a "good" system.[12]

These same sociologists have recognized how patterns of juvenile delinquency can be attributed to sex-typed, near-ritualistic behavior. But this observation has not led them to realize the need of reducing cultural emphasis on sexism. Studies on conflict in the traditional nuclear family, or on stifled personality development in the family, have not led to any large-scale critique of the family in texts on "family and marriage." Sociologists have addressed themselves to inherently conservative questions, for they assume that it is desirable to "adjust" within the nuclear family pattern. They do not usually consider the possibility of alternative living arrangements, except under the rubric of deviancy.

No distinct sociological discipline has existed to study sex-typing as one dimension of social stratification. This is another reflection of the way in which scholars and academicians join other elites to perpetuate the status quo. Sociologists are no more likely than businessmen or craftsmen to recognize that sexual "discrimination" exists, much less that it is a problem. In their own profession, the proportion of women is far less than the proportion of women in the labor market as a whole. At recent professional meetings, promises to rectify some of these conditions were made, but sociologists have shown no overwhelming inclination to make good those promises.

Anthropologists have done more than sociologists in exploring relationships among women and men cross-culturally.

12. Talcott Parsons and Robert F. Bales et al., *Family, Socialization and Interaction Process* (Glencoe, Ill.: The Free Press, 1955, 1960).

The conclusions that are drawn from such research, however, are often based on the acceptance of psychoanalytic theory. Even after formally denouncing such theory, one anthropologist asserts:

> Physiologically there exists a passionate instinctive interest of the mother in the child . . . Yet even here in a relation so fundamental, so biologically secured, there are certain societies where custom and laxity of innate impulses allow of notable aberrations. Thus we have the system of sending the child away for the first year or so of life to a hired foster mother . . . or the almost equally harmful system of protecting the woman's breasts by hiring a foster mother, or by feeding the child on artificial food, a custom once prevalent among the wealthy classes, though today generally stigmatized as unnatural.[13]

Notice the tendency to define what is "natural" and what is "aberrant" simply by reference to the author's own cultural preferences and wishes. The inability of some biological mothers to enthusiastically assume the mothering role to which they are assigned is sufficient evidence to call into question all of the interpretations made by scholars such as this one. In explaining the "fathering" behavior of Trobriand Islanders, this same scholar makes no reference to "instinct" or "nature":

> Among the Melanesians "fatherhood," as we know, is a purely social relation . . . The typical Trobriand father is a hard-working and conscientious nurse . . . always interested in the children, sometimes passionately so, and he performs all his duties eagerly and fondly.[14]

13. Bronislaw Malinowski, *Sex and Repression in Savage Society* (New York: The World Publishing Company, 1927, 1968), pp. 29, 31.
14. *Ibid.*, p. 33.

Within the academic professions, there is no assurance that women will be any more willing than men to recognize the discrepancies in interpretation and the cultural biases that result from sexism. Academic women are under strong pressures to conform. As members of an extreme minority, they generally assume roles within their professions that do not permit them to speak or write as theoreticians or as authorities.

THE MARKETPLACE

The separation of men and women, besides being useful as a means of assuring their easy availability as laborers to those who profit from their services, is useful in creating a demand for endless production of goods by casting men as "providers" and women as "consumers" and baby-machines so that the economy is assured of expansion (and eventual extinction!) by an ever-increasing population. To serve these ends, Madison Avenue joins forces with other "social experts" in selling sexism to the public.

The process begins as soon as children are old enough to watch television. Today's child, in the United States, watches television on the average from four to six hours a day. Little girls are shown in advertisements as clean and sweet and reactive. They are, in effect, understudies for their mothers who are homemakers, or for their teen-age counterparts who are sexual objects, sophisticated or demure, career-girl (secretary, stewardess, etc.), or socialite. Little boys are shown as competition-oriented, power-hungry, active, and forgiveable—understudies for the soldier, the Casanova, the producer.

The G.I. Joe "action figure" and the Barbie "doll," together with the story material that accompanies them, have out-advertised all other products in the past fifteen years. One toy manufacturer claims to have increased the company advertising budget to fifteen times the earlier advertising budget of the entire toy industry. Most of this expenditure is for television commercials.

The adult roles that children see on television are no less stereotyped. Rarely do children see women making important decisions or men taking orders from women in either commercials or programs—except as a comedy in which the incongruity of the situation is made evident. "Straight," "wholesome" fare demands that human complexities be avoided. If not, they are presented as "unnatural" behavior that is then resolved at the end of the story by the acceptance of social norms.

Daytime, weekday television is geared exclusively to women, and principally to women's roles as consumers, while Saturday morning television is geared largely to young boys.

One study showed a preponderance of toy advertisements directed to boys exclusively. The sponsors' motivations for such programming might be that boys' toys are usable for girls as well, while the reverse is not true in a male-dominant culture. Thus, it is more profitable to advertise these. An alternative explanation is that parents are thought to be willing to spend more on young boys than on young girls. This is perhaps a more likely possibility since studies show that parents give little boys more time and attention than little girls.

An example of blatant appeal to sexism in the mass media is provided in this ad shown on television by a local furniture company:

> When you live with the same furniture for ten or fifteen years . . . you grow so accustomed to it, you don't see it

as others do . . . for instance like your well-to-do neighbor
sees it . . . who's just refurnished her big home across the
street . . . or the way your mother sees it who's always tried
to impress on your husband that a daughter of hers deserves
more than just the bare necessities. Maybe it's time you
started looking at your furniture as *others* do. Because *others*
do.[15]

The home and wife as status symbols in the nature of
"conspicuous consumption" are only one aspect of the emphasis on female glamor. Women are made to feel they
must give special attention to their bodies in order to increase their desirability to men—a custom reminiscent of
the purification rites required of women in other parts of
the world. A widely televised series of advertisements links
the use of personal hygiene products with the possibility of
winning a man, and shows a wedding scene as the "happy
ending" for users of these products.

A sense of inadequacy in oneself—dehumanization—no
doubt accompanies the extreme focusing on makeup and
hygiene and learning the mannerisms of the "feminine role."
One wonders what changes in men will accompany the contemporary efforts by Madison Avenue to draw them into
a "male glamor" role.

A culture that is dominated by the mass media, or more
specifically, a mass media controlled by business interests,
seems to assure that *things* will be more heavily emphasized
than meaningful human relationships. Sexism lends itself
perfectly to this emphasis. A woman is encouraged to regard
her kitchen floors and her white sheets as an extension of
herself, and a man is encouraged to regard his car as an
extension of himself.

The mass media perpetuate the culture of sexism in many

15. Channel 4, WWJ—TV (Detroit, Winter, 1969).

ways, but none is more obvious than the Woman's Section in newspapers. By implication, other sections of the newspapers deal with the areas of life over which women have little or no control. In the same vein are special features such as "Men on the Make" (listing promotions of prominent persons), and "Working Girl of the Week" (girl, not woman), and the generalized use of the male gender in addressing letters to the editor. Although listing job opportunities by sex has been declared unconstitutional, this practice still persists in most newspapers.

Much of the asexual content of cultural teaching is in fact directed toward men. The worship of the gun in American entertainment media can be interpreted as male fetishism and repressed sexuality; the competitiveness that keeps the economic system running is billed as a major component of manliness; the superpatriotism that characterizes foreign policy propaganda can be seen as a "defense of masculinity." These attitudes are not instilled without intensive and continuous effort.

In spite of unprecedented expense, however, and with maximum attention to the "sexual sell," it has been impossible for United States government-subsidized manufacturers of toy guns and war games to sustain the "war toy craze" that peaked in 1964–65. It should certainly raise some serious questions about the "naturalness" (if not necessity) of sex-role differences when one realizes how much effort is required (and even then, with limited success) to "keep people in their places."

In summary the lure of rewards such as honor and prestige, or the threat of punishments such as ridicule or eternal damnation, are the principal means of controlling social behavior. These find systematic expression in the mass media, the schools, and the churches. None of our institutions are immune from the sexism that is so much a part of our culture. But religion, science, and entertainment impinge on our lives as agencies of social control in ways that are so pervasive and subtle that careful research and constant watchfulness are necessary to loosen their grip and make change possible.

REFERENCES

CAROL ANDREAS, "War Toys and the Peace Movement," *Journal of Social Issues*, XXV, *1*, 1969; reprinted in simplified form in ASA paperback on Mass Behavior, for high school use.

JESSE BERNARD, *Academic Women*, University Park, Pennsylvania: The Pennsylvania State University Press, 1964.

EDMUND DAHLSTROM, *The Changing Roles of Men and Women*, London: Gerald Duckworth & Co. Ltd., 1967.

MARY DALY, *The Church and the Second Sex*, New York: Harper & Row, Publishers, 1968.

MARY ELLMAN, *Thinking About Women*, New York: Harcourt Brace Jovanovich, Inc., 1968.

WILLIAM J. GOODE, *Women in Divorce*, New York: The Free Press, 1956.

VIOLA KLEIN, *The Feminine Character*, London: Routledge & Kegan Paul Ltd., Trench, Trubner & Co., Ltd., 1946, Chapter V.

LAWRENCE LANGER, *The Importance of Wearing Clothes*, New York: Hastings House, 1959, p. 55.

KATE MILLETT, *Sexual Politics*, New York: Doubleday & Company Inc., 1970.

CYNTHIA OZICK, "The Demise of the Dancing Dog," *Motive*, 6 and 7, p. 9.

NAOMI WEISSTEIN, "Kinder, Kuche, Kirche as scientific law; Psychology Constructs the female," *Sisterhood is Powerful*, Robin Morgan, ed., New York: Random House, Inc., 1970.

"Sex Roles in Television Commercials," class project at Oakland University, Winter 1969, Carol Andreas, instructor (copy on file at Women's Liberation Coalition Office, Detroit).

5

LAWS AND MORALS:
The Sins of Commission

Everyone agrees that society has a stake in the lives of its members. But what exactly do we mean by such a statement? Does the society have a stake only in the survival of its members, in their happiness, in their productivity, in their wealth, in their obedience? The answer must surely depend on the nature and composition of its ruling group.

MARRIAGE AND THE FAMILY

When the base of a society's economic system is capitalism, and especially when its political base is some form of oligarchy, whether formally "representative" or not, it is likely to depend on the nuclear family to maintain the concept of property rights and to socialize or train individuals to accept hierarchical relations between people. The nuclear family, in contrast with extended families of kin, for instance, also makes possible a certain amount of geographic mobility from city to city and from job to job. It places the burden of care of the young, the poor, the ill, and the aged on individuals rather than on the larger family or community group. Thus, individuals are motivated to work, consume, accumulate, and behave politically in ways that are most likely to maintain a competitive economic system.

Although these possibilities may not be very adequately realized, their importance for the continuation of a competitive social order is nevertheless clear. For this reason, it should not be surprising that in societies such as the United States, the doctrine of laissez faire—the old "let them alone" policy of classical capitalism—is not applied to relations between the sexes. Speaking of legal aspects of marriage, the author of a widely-used textbook declares:

> However much these regulations would seem to impinge on the right of the participants, it is clear that society cannot adopt a *laissez faire* attitude toward the institution of marriage. There is too much at stake . . . In modern civilization, where property rights and inheritance are so important, formal regulation of marriage becomes a necessity . . . The state has a vested interest in the legitimacy of children and the protection of women; if the male is not held to be legally responsible for the support of his wife and children, the burden must ultimately fall upon society at large.[1]

The author goes on to describe how the state becomes most directly involved in marriage. Private contracts, unlike marriage contracts, can be modified or broken by mutual consent. They can be drawn for two parties irrespective of their color and blood ties, and only if the parties are adults. None of these conditions necessarily holds true of the marriage contract. The contract can only be broken with the consent of the state, and only if some violation of law has occurred to make the marriage void or voidable. Marriage can occur only between persons who are considered suitable

1. William Kephart, *The Family, Society, and the Individual* (Boston: Houghton Mifflin Company, 1961, 1966), pp. 376–77.

for procreation with each other according to the prejudices of the particular state or region, and it can take place between minors so long as they have the consent of their parents.

Therefore, says the author, it is particularly dangerous for the state to recognize common-law marriages, in which special provisions regarding marriage cannot be enforced.

> Custom per se cannot turn wrong into right. The fact of the matter is that common-law marriage has long since outlived its usefulness . . . society loses much of its control over specific marital prohibitions . . . Common-law marriages . . . devoid as they generally are of documentary proof . . . tend to snarl the machinery of the court. This is especially true in decisions involving inheritance rights . . . Our licensing and recording procedures enable us to compile valuable statistical information regarding marriage and divorce in the United States. The prevalence of common-law marriage upsets, to an unknown degree, all of the available figures, since a non-licensed marriage is neither recorded nor reported . . . There can be little doubt that common-law marriage is a social evil. In due time, perhaps, such marriages will be outlawed by all of the states. Lawyers and bar association groups have been advocating such a measure for many years.[2]

Similar writers claim that it is difficult to think of any benefit that is gained by the continued recognition of common-law marriage by one-third of the states in the United States. Obviously they are not interested in finding out whether or not such marriages improve the quality of the relationships involved. Human happiness is often given little priority in judging the benefits versus costs of a social cus-

2. *Ibid.*, pp. 397–400.

tom. The convenience of lawyers and of government bureaucrats is apparently more worthy of consideration.

While concerned about the continuing practice of common-law marriage, textbooks have shown little concern about the prohibition of interracial marriage, a clearly unconstitutional law.[3] Even the principle of reciprocity has been waived in the case of marriage between different racial groups, so that couples who became legally married in one state have been apprehended for living together in another. Among the nineteen states where marriage between blacks and whites was forbidden as recently as 1967 are Wyoming and Indiana —two states that are not located in the South where racial prejudice is presumed to be strongest. In other Northern states, it is not uncommon for a white mother to lose custody of her children following divorce if she subsequently marries a black.

Minimum age requirements for marriage also reflect state and regional differences, although in any locality a judge or other qualified official may entirely waive age requirements if pregnancy is involved. In every state, the minimum age for marriage with consent and the minimum age for marriage without consent are both younger for women than for men, a device quite obviously calculated to facilitate dominance of the man in the marriage relationship.

Marriages may be declared void, in which case annulment may be granted, or they may be merely voidable, in which case separation, divorce, or separate maintenance may occur. In the case of void marriages, the societal interest is presumed to be directly at stake. In the case of voidable marriages, one of the spouses is presumed to be the victim of

3. The case of *Loving versus Virginia* tested the constitutionality of laws barring interracial marriage in 1967.

the other, and the outcome is left to the discretion of the courts. Grounds for divorce vary from one state to another and there is little relationship between the nature of the marital discord and the official reasons given for divorce. Litigation nearly always involves a certain amount of subterfuge, which intensifies the conflict between the spouses. Litigation, of course, involves money, so wealthy parties have access to benefits not available to the poor.

Near the turn of the century, when the divorce rate was rising rapidly, legislation was introduced in many states to make divorce more difficult, but such legislation usually failed to pass. At that time, two-thirds of the divorces were initiated by women. The rising divorce rate was attributed to their loss of piety, engendered by feminist thinking. The debate over abolishing divorce was carried on largely in the churches, and was lost by those who wanted to preserve the sanctity of marriage largely because they were split over details.

Radical proponents of divorce tended to see the issue as part of a larger movement toward free love and socialism. They failed to understand that, far from being a threat to the nuclear family, the rising divorce rate contributed to its strength and stability as a social institution in an era of rising expectations for companionship between marital partners. The provisions for continued support of women and children by men following divorce assure that important features of the marriage system are preserved. The inability of women to make a place for themselves in the society, or to fulfill their sexual needs legitimately as "unattached" women assures that they will remarry as soon as possible. In most cases, property settlements favor the man and custody of children is almost automatically given to the woman. Again, this assures that important features of the system are kept intact. Custody has recently been denied women on grounds of immorality or for political reasons in cases where women have participated actively in the Womens' Liberation Movement. Alternative life styles such as communal living are not available to men and women who want to assure that their children will not become political pawns.

With or without divorce, the family is often the scene of intense conflict. One-fourth of all homicides for instance, occur among family members, and untold numbers of suicides, beatings, and assaults stem from family disputes. It is likely that many marriages last for years not because of family solidarity but because of the existence of extreme coercive conditions.

In each of these instances, the state's interest is not primarily in the happiness of its constituents, but rather, in preserving certain institutionalized features of their lives.

CONTROL OF REPRODUCTION

The interest in preserving the traditional order is nowhere more clearly illustrated than in attitudes toward abortion, and more generally, toward birth control. Since the beginnings of Judaeo-Christian morality in Western civilization, women have seldom been allowed to exercise control over their own reproductive functions, and they have been mercilessly punished or stigmatized for doing so. The patriarchal order demands that "woman's place is in the home." It demands further that child-bearing and child-rearing be highly regarded occupations for women—indeed, these activities must be synonymous with virtue. The Catholic

Church subordinates all other functions of marriage to the function of procreation, and all other functions of women to that of mothering. The restrictions placed on women to prevent pregnancy or development of the fetus are certainly not attributable to any pacific concern for the sacredness of human life in general—there is no generalized prohibition on taking human life. In fact, those religious groups which are most pacific are least dogmatic about restricting women from controlling their own reproductive activities.

Abortion and contraceptive legislation is currently in a state of flux, because of pressures being brought to bear on state legislatures, and at various governmental levels throughout the world. A detailed description of such laws would therefore not be very helpful. It is important to point out, however, that everywhere husbands can be readily sterilized without permission from their wives, but wives cannot have their reproductive organs modified in any way without the written approval of their husbands. The extent of illegal activity in this area is, of course, phenomenal. It is the center of a controversy which has so far failed to produce any radical changes in the United States. Reforms, even to the extent of repeal of legislation that makes abortion illegal, do little to rectify a situation that makes voluntary abortion available only to the wealthy, and involuntary abortion more likely for the poor.

In those European and Asian countries where free and legal abortions are available, however, public opinion and practice has shown a surprising degree of resilience, not to mention the consequent reduction in population growth and in death rates for mothers and infants.

NON-MARITAL SEX

Among the many aspects of relations between the sexes in which the state has an interest, marriage and the family is only one. The other side of the coin is the prohibition of numerous extramarital relations between men and women, which are thereby labelled not only deviant, but also criminal. Needless to say, most of these prohibitions are unenforced and unenforceable, but they serve, nevertheless, to further legitimize marriage and the family. They also serve to degrade those who, for profit or pleasure, wish to be free from the restrictions of marriage and family.

Such degradation is felt far more strongly by women than by men, partly because of the visibility of an unwanted pregnancy (women are often loathe to make their plights even more public by declaring paternity). Women have the greater burden also because the state is far more concerned with the societal burden which such pregnancies represent than with the morality of extramarital sex itself. The sterilization of unwed fathers has never been suggested as a remedy for the birth of children out of wedlock, although a number of states have attempted to enact such legislation for unwed mothers. Poor black women in America have long complained of unwanted sterilizations and abortions.

Another reason why the degradation of nonmarital sex falls more heavily on women is the fact that they are generally disadvantaged in the labor market. They can partially redress this difference by using sex for monetary gain. The sex act has been structured by society, even within marriage, to provide tangible gain for the woman, and to provide either a sense of conquest or satisfaction of a "natural right" for the man. Thus, prostitution is more likely to be practiced by women who need money and solicited by men who lack success in competition or fulfillment in marriage. Again, the solicitor is less visible than the prostitute, and, thus, less subject to censure.

Among those who profit directly or indirectly from prostitution are cabdrivers and bellhops, abortionists, attorneys, "medical examiners," policemen, "fixers," prosecutors, judges, bail bondsmen, and, in some cases, hiring agents, hotel managers, bar owners, and drug peddlers. The prostitute is especially vulnerable because she is prohibited from organizing at the rank-and-file level to protect her own interests. Convictions for prostitution are often made on the strength of an officer's statement, resulting in a judicial process that has been likened to a taxation procedure.

In the case of homosexuality, the degradation suffered by men is greater than that suffered by women. Laws reflect this difference, often prohibiting sexual liaisons between men but not between women. To recognize lesbianism in women would be to admit that women have sexual needs, and that they are not merely objects to be used to satisfy men's needs. Similarly, rape is defined as a crime that men commit against women, so that the possibility of a sex drive in women, which could conceivably express itself in a coercive way, is effectively denied. Men who are members of minority groups can suffer extreme penalties for allegedly raping women belonging to majority groups; they are quite helpless in defending themselves against such charges.

According to one author, society saves its greatest wrath for those who violate the norms of sexual propriety through incest and/or child molestation:

> If homosexuality offers the greatest stigma, rape the greatest potential for arousing ethnic passions, incest the severest repulsion and revulsion, then the sexual advance of an adult

to a child probably brings forth fear and anger in the adult world most out of proportion to the potential injury to the child. If anything, in fact, the child seems often to be injured more by the reaction of parents and authorities than by the act itself.[4]

In all of these instances, just as in the case of laws regulating pornography and deviant sexual acts even within marriage, the net result of legal repression is to make sexual conduct outside of accepted patterns seem dangerous or evil. This then heightens the guilt or anxiety among those who are judged to indulge their sexual appetites indiscriminately, i.e., in ways not conducive to preservation of the patriarchal family as the foundation of the social order.[5] Were such legal repression actually carried out consistently, however, the institution of marriage would be even more seriously threatened, since these aberrations serve as safety valves for a less than perfectly satisfying institution.

Nowhere is this more true, perhaps, than in the case of adultery, where laws that are officially on the books are almost never applied. In the case of adultery, however, crimes of passion against a wayward spouse are sometimes excused, or recognized as a separate category, for men but not for women. In some places, a single instance of adultery on the part of the wife is grounds for divorce; but a wife is entitled to divorce only if her husband abandons her to live with another woman.

Encouragement for legal marriage is provided in many subtle ways, not the least of which is the income tax advan-

4. Edward Sagarin and Donald MacNamara, eds., *Problems of Sex Behavior* (New York: Thomas Y. Crowell Company, 1968), p. 242.

5. Wilhelm Reich has developed in his writings the thesis that sexual repression and patriarchal structures are necessary components of fascist rule over individuals. See, for instance, *Sexual Revolution* (New York: Farrar, Strauss and Cudahy, 1969).

tage for married couples, and the insurance and pension benefits available only to them. Within marriage, however, women lose many rights that they would otherwise have, such as the right to select a place of residence, the right to separate domicile (except in specified situations, as during divorce litigation), and the right to transact business independently.

Poor women experience a different sort of pressure, being "damned if they do (marry) and damned if they don't." They can usually receive welfare payments only if they are neither married nor enjoying the company of a man. Such contradictions cannot fail to generate pressures for change, such as the current collective efforts of welfare mothers. This struggle, which has continued for nearly a decade, can in some ways be interpreted as the vanguard of the contemporary Women's Liberation Movement.

DISCRIMINATION IN THE LEGAL PROCESS

The law effectively dictates the limits of what is to be officially tolerated in a society. But the judicial process is complex. The ways in which men and women are involved in this process is another important area in which sex differences are prevalent.

Women are eligible to serve on federal juries under the Civil Rights Act of 1957. But in three states, women are not invited to serve on juries of the state courts. In more than half the states, women called for jury service may claim exemptions for which men are not eligible. And since jury lists are derived from voting registrants, minorities who do not feel themselves to be part of the formal political system cannot possibly be tried by a jury of "peers."

Many sexually discriminatory practices are enshrined in various state and local laws, such as those prohibiting women from standing at the bar in public places or from operating bars, and those restricting the hours and working conditions for women. In most such legislation, the ostensible purpose is to *protect* women. However, such protection can delimit their freedom and their ability to compete with men for higher positions and rewards.

On such issues as overtime restrictions, the answer would seem to be for overtime work to be made voluntary for both men and women. Few businesses have so far been willing to accept that principle, and since unions, over the years, have tended to accept management principles developed in large corporations, only wildcat strikes and other opposition forces within these organizations have pushed for more flexible working conditions. Title VII of the Civil Rights Act of 1964 has so far been interpreted to mean that protections should be available to neither females nor males.

Passage of further equal rights legislation pertaining to sex, unless such legislation includes provisions for extension of existing protective legislation to include men, could be used to make conditions worse for many working women. They would then be subject to abusive practices such as involuntary overtime and assembly-line speed-ups. Passage of an equal rights amendment, which would safeguard men and women from such abuses, would, however, be a major victory for workers. It would give priority to human needs— above the needs of the corporate owners to utilize labor in whatever way is most efficient for production (or profit).

Even if such legislation is enacted, enforcement is another matter. Until such time as workers demand to choose their own bosses, and until such time as women are given an equal voice with men in workers' organizations, they are not likely to experience humane working conditions. Today's labor unions are not moving in either of these directions.

The Women's Equity Action League has called for action to be taken under Executive Order 11246 as amended by E.O. 11375 (1967) which prohibits discrimination on the part of organizations holding contracts with the federal government. They have met with some success in the withholding of at least one contract from a large state university. But this did not occur until university women made and documented specific charges. The governmental investigative committee initially claimed that it was not empowered to do more than investigate such specific charges.

The American Sociological Association, at its 1970 convention, voted to provide legal funds for the womens' caucus to bring pressure on sociology departments that discriminate against women. In the face of widespread discrimination, the unanimous passage of such resolutions, without debate, seems ludicrous if not pathetic. But it does demonstrate the unwillingness of professional men to expose their feelings in such matters.

Clearly, there have been some significant changes in the sexual order since the colonial days when "witches" and homosexuals were burned at the stake in America, when women and children were completely at the mercy of their factory employers, and when women were sold at public auction. Today, men are probably as likely as women to be singled out for persecution because of political or religious heresy or because of repudiating customary dress styles. Marriages are contracted with the mutual consent of the parties involved. It is not so frightening any more to see women assuming prerogatives formerly granted only to men. And, as we have seen, the occupational *caste* system operates in a less pervasive manner, so that roles that are masculine in one location may be feminine in another.

In some respects, custom has moved more rapidly than law in breaking down barriers to human freedom. Where people have disagreed about the direction of change, power struggles have determined legislation.

ENACTMENT OF LAWS FAVORING EGALITARIAN NORMS

So far, only restrictive laws have been discussed, those which prohibit behavior that threatens the traditional patriarchal family system. There are other laws, however, enacted mainly during the past fifty years, that are designed to change the sexual order as it was traditionally defined, to make possible at least a modicum of equality of opportunity. Since the progressive era of reform, there has been a tendency to officially encourage egalitarianism between men and women, as among all citizens, at least in certain spheres.

After decades of struggle, the sphere of politics has been changed legislatively to conform with the rhetoric of equality. The fact remains, however, that it would not have been necessary to spell out the eligibility of both men and women for participation in government had it been assumed that they were. The legalization of suffrage for women has not noticeably affected their participation as equals at all levels of government.

The same is true in the economic sphere. With the passage of the Fair Labor Standards Act, as amended by the Equal Pay Act in 1963, for instance, there were renewed attempts to control the behavior of women through noncoercive means —such as the effort by Presidential Advisor Patrick Moynihan to castigate black women for assuming dominance in their homes and communities and men for allowing them to do so.

The completion, in 1965, of the Report of the President's Commission on the Status of Women—with its specific recommendations for legislative changes to assure an improvement in the opportunities available to women (if not equality of opportunity)—was a sign of increasing official sanction for changes in sex-role behavior. However, the present administration has so far shown little inclination to continue in this direction. The second task force report was withheld from the public for six months until women's pressure groups forced it to be published in 1970.

Among the most effective ways to keep women at home is to see that there are few facilities available for the care of children. After World War II, the closing of government child care centers in the United States forced significant numbers of working women to return to their domestic roles. In the late 1960s, renewed efforts have been made to subsidize day care for children with federal funds. Most of such funding could be provided by one of the programs instituted by the War on Poverty begun by the Kennedy administration. But this funding is subject to annual review and it is available only to children from poor homes. Therefore, it is difficult to say whether or not general acceptance of child care programs will increase, or even whether growth will actually occur in the availability of such services.

Even when funds are made available, the restrictions on the operation of child care facilities often discourage the most capable men and women from seeking staff positions in them. Such restrictions reflect a welfare-state mentality that views state-supported child care as an obligation of the rich toward the poor, where poor unmarried women are *required* to place their children in such facilities to make themselves available as cheap labor, and middle- and upper-class women are encouraged to seek such services only as a poor substitute for the home. This mentality exists in spite of a great deal of cross-cultural and experimental data that point to the many benefits of multiple mothering, of child development in a peer-group setting, and of improvement of parent-child relationships when both parents are pursuing work of their own choosing.[6]

As long as the child care programs are thought appropriate only for the children of the poor, there is not likely to be widespread change in sex role behavior. For women to be devoted to *House and Garden,* and to the care of their own children within the confines of the nuclear family, will continue to be a mark of prestige. Even such facilities as are available to working mothers seldom include provision for care of infants, provision for night-time care, or for after school care for older children. And most child care programs inculcate traditional sex-role habits and attitudes in children, and make no attempt to desegregate their own staffs.

In some communities, young people, parents and non-parents, are caring for children cooperatively without seeking a state license to do so. If this trend becomes widespread, state laws may be forced to change. With the growth of communal life-styles in the United States, it is possible that some form of recognition of "common-law parentage" will eventually occur, although such a development will not come without struggle and sacrifice. Local zoning boards, for instance, are noted for political corruption; housing laws are slow to change. And both are presently supportive of traditional family arrangements.

An alternative to community-controlled child care is the expansion of child care services that are operated for profit,

6. Ivan Nye and Lois Hoffman, eds., *The Employed Mother in America* (Chicago: Rand McNally and Company, 1963).

or otherwise controlled by monied interests either through private franchises or by corporations or governmental bureaucracies. The effects of such services are not to liberate human beings but to use them. Wherever funding from government or business sources is sought, parents will have to insist on their own right to control policy and staffing.

Reporting on a conference of businessmen and educators held in New York City during the summer of 1970, members of a Boston Child Care Action Group write:

> Wall Street's man, from Dominick & Dominick, said he had a hobby of following education. He said, "the education area was the last remaining capital intensive industry to put the whole kit and kaboodle into perspective." He did see some "significant long term thrust" but for now the day care business would have to earn some "brownie points" in the next three or four years to prove their "viability to the market." He said that given the tightness of the market these days, day care businesses would be best to look to venture capital. The "software market," (product packages, franchises) looked better than the "hard-ware" (toys, materials). He foresees that "exciting new trends in educational machinery" will cut expenses since 90% of the operating costs in day care seem to revolve around personnel. One tape deck he had heard about "might be a very cheap way of putting Mother Goose or whatever else you wanted" across to the kids, thereby cutting out the need for so many teachers.[7]

Change in America will have to proceed very rapidly to head off the usurpation of child care by such people. There is danger, also, that public schools will undertake to include the care of younger children in their programs. Although adequate child care programs in the United States would

7. *Off Our Backs*, 1, 9 and 10 (Washington, D.C., 1970): 5.

cost at least ten billion dollars annually, and although public funds ought to be made available for this purpose, the schools are already so thoroughly committed to serving the needs of corporations and other powerful groupings in the society that their ability to give priority to the needs of children is extremely doubtful.

Several cases, in which desegregation of educational institutions was at issue, have come before the courts very recently. In addition to a modification of admission requirements, there is some emphasis, especially on college campuses, on relaxing the double standards that have characterized dormitory regulations. Dormitory regulations do not have the force of law, and they can be challenged quite effectively by collective action on the part of students. Students have demanded, with increasing success, desegregation of dormitories and easing of regulations pertaining to visiting times.

Students who are most disadvantaged today are those who prefer homosexual to heterosexual relationships. Such students are likely to be heavily censured or expelled from school. Public activity on the part of homosexuals—who have begun to hold gay dances in university facilities and to educate student populations about the normalcy of their behavior—is an attempt to deal constructively with the problems of homosexuals, or of those who would like to encourage bisexuality.

Increasingly, there is agreement among people who oppose sexism that egalitarian norms will only be possible when homosexuality and bisexuality are completely legitimized. This would mean enactment of "model criminal codes" (already under discussion in a number of state legislatures), which would make legal any sexual acts performed in private by consenting adults. It would also mean realizing such behavior in daily conduct and relaxing the repressive demands made upon children.

On the college campus, such a relaxation of sexual codes would make possible the development of warm and sincere human relationships as a complement to the development of intellectual and aesthetic skills. It would counteract anxieties and frantic efforts to "be popular" or to "be powerful" while trying, at the same time, to learn scholarly habits and decide vocational commitments.

In the period of young adulthood, men are faced with another blatant violation of civil rights pertaining to sex— the drafting of young men for military service. It is now being challenged for the first time in a court of law. Until recently, widespread protests against the draft have not been defined as a sex-role issue. This lack of consciousness resulted from an unwillingness to give up other features of the sexual *caste* system that are beneficial to men. Now that women are challenging these benefits, men are more likely to express their own resentments in areas where they suffer most from sex-role expectations.

A strong case can be made that the drafting of anyone for military service is a gross violation of civil rights, especially if they are not represented in Congress—as young men and women are not. Therefore, it may not be useful to argue about the sex biases involved (and certainly not about the lack of opportunities for females to advance within the military bureaucracy). But as long as there is a draft, questions must inevitably be raised about the basis on which draftees are "chosen." The presence of large numbers of female soldiers in the regular armies of Israel, in the Vietnam and Palestine liberation forces, and in a few scattered areas elsewhere, makes the question more than academic. In such cases, the role of women in the armed services is still not identical to that of men, but arbitrary divisions are at least being challenged. Women do assume heavy responsibilities in the front lines.

It is reasonable to predict that the numbers of legal complaints pertaining to sex discrimination will continue to increase in the United States and around the globe. Some of the cases involved will reach the highest courts. In some instances, legal changes are bound to give an appearance of egalitarianism with little substance, as in the case of revision of divorce legislation in California.[8] Should this become clear to those victimized by *caste*, it will no doubt lead to renewed militancy in the social sphere.

ACTIVITIES OF THE UNITED NATIONS

Renewed organizational efforts to equalize the opportunities of men and women may not be focussed only within nations. Some efforts may continue and increase to secure more widespread ratification of the Universal Declarations on Human Rights pertaining to sex, as passed by the General Assembly of the United Nations. Only a few member nations have ratified these declarations; there continues to be debate on the rights of member states to maintain their own "cultural differences" in this area.

United Nations conventions do not have the force of law, but they do represent an ideal toward which member states are expected to strive in their own legislation and social customs. So far, legislative bodies in the United States have not been put under pressure by any powerful groups to ratify the conventions, which include the following:

1. The 1952 convention on the political rights of women

8. Leo Kanowitz, *Women and the Law: The Unfinished Revolution* (Albuquerque: University of New Mexico Press, 1969).

2. The 1957 convention on the nationality of married women

3. The 1962 convention on consent to marriage, minimum age for marriage, and registration of marriages, and the 1965 recommendation on the same subject

4. The 1951 International Labour Organization (ILO) convention on equal remuneration for men and women workers of equal value

5. The 1958 ILO discrimination (occupational and employment) convention

6. The 1960 United Nations Educational, Scientific, and Cultural Organization (UNESCO) convention and recommendation against discrimination in education

7. The general statement in which all members were invited to prepare long-term programs at the national level, including, as a first step, urgent measures to be taken in the ten-year period beginning in 1968

One result of the UN activity in these areas was the appointment, by President John F. Kennedy, of Eleanor Roosevelt as chairwoman of the President's Commission on the Status of Women in the United States. No similar effort of this magnitude had been undertaken since 1920, when President Woodrow Wilson established a Women's Bureau in the Department of Labor.

Citizens of the United States should be aware that they are not in the vanguard on these matters. In this country, and particularly in the area of legislation regarding marriage, the following comment is almost as true today as it was many years ago:

> The wives of humane, affectionate husbands and the slaves of kind, considerate masters scarcely noticed the legal restraints put upon them, but on the wives and slaves of fickle, ignorant, and brutal husbands and masters, always

numerous, the oppression of the law fell with crushing force. . . .[9]

THE POLITICAL POWER OF WOMEN IN AMERICA

Laws are, as has often been said, made by men, and quite literally so. Laws are also interpreted by men. The paucity of women jurors has already been noted. In the law profession, the absence of women is even more remarkable. At a recent meeting of the American Trial Lawyers Association, one observer reported seeing no women among the several hundred participating members. Among corporation lawyers, discrimination is reportedly even more severe than among trial lawyers.

Most lawyers are members of law firms. The few women who do manage to survive their period of education in a field not noted for giving encouragement to women are likely to be assigned to research or semi-clerical tasks within the firms that admit them. Whether women lawyers and law students who are currently struggling for fair treatment within their profession will achieve their goals—short of an overall change in the productive relations of men and women in the society—seems unlikely. But any progress made in this area will no doubt have an effect out of proportion to the numbers of women involved.

The numbers of women in positions of political power in the United States stands in sharp contrast to the status of women in those countries where recent social revolutions have been attempted. In the U.S.S.R., for instance, where

9. Carrie Chapman Catt, as quoted by Margaret Bruce, "An Account of United Nations Action to Advance the Status of Women," *The Annals of the American Academy of Political and Social Science,* 375 (January, 1968): 169–70.

women were once kept out of political life altogether unless they were able to exercise power through family connections, women today occupy twenty-eight percent of the seats in the Supreme Council and forty-two percent of the positions in local councils. The Supreme Court of the U.S.S.R. is forty percent women, and the People's Courts, thirty-one percent. No other modern nation-state can claim such wide participation by women in the formal political process.

The proportion of women in such positions of power in the United States is still miniscule. There has never been a woman Supreme Court judge. Today, there is only one woman senator. Women in the House of Representatives compose only 2.3 percent of that body. One study estimated that forty of the 1400 top political jobs in the United States are held by women. At state and local levels, opportunities for women are restricted, no less than at the federal level, by lack of money, by systematic discrimination in both major parties, and by the kind of "modesty" that derives from the traditional woman's role.

Given women's status in our society, discriminated against in law and social practices, it is understandable that members of the Women's Liberation Movement are demanding that women now serving jail sentences for shoplifting, prostitution, and truancy should be recognized as political prisoners and freed until such time as sexist laws and sexist customs are eliminated.

REFERENCES

ROBERT BELL, *Marriage and Family Interaction*, Homewood, Illinois: The Dorsey Press, 1967.

BRUNO BETTLEHEIM, *Children of the Dream: Communal Child-Rearing and American Education*, London: MacMillan Co. Ltd., 1969.

URIE BRONFENBRENNER, *Two Worlds of Childhood: U.S. and U.S.S.R.*, New York: Russell Sage Foundation, 1970.

PHILIP FRANCIS, *The Legal Status of Women*, New York: Oceana, 1963.

Voices of the New Feminism (Friedan, Koontz, Chisholm, Dunbar, Griffiths, Bird, Murray, Daly, Pullen, Rossi, Cowley, Cisler, Thompson), Boston, Massachusetts: Beacon Press. 1970.

P. MAGINNIS and L. C. PHALEN, *Abortion Handbook for Responsible Women*, North Hollywood, California: Contact Books, 1969.

MARGARET MEAD and FRANCES KAPLAN, eds., *American Women, Report of the President's Commission*, New York: Charles Scribner's Sons, 1965.

NANCY MILIO, *9226 Kercheval: The Storefront That Did Not Burn*, Ann Arbor, Michigan: University of Michigan Press, 1970.

WILLIAM O'NEILL, *Divorce in the Progressive Era*, New Haven, Connecticut: Yale University Press, 1967.

HARRIET PILPEL and THEODORA ZAVIN, *Your Marriage and the Law*, New York: Collier Books, 1952, 1964.

MORRIS PLOSCOWE, *Sex and the Law*, Englewood Cliffs, New Jersey: Prentice-Hall, Inc., 1951.

HAROLD ROSEN, ed., *Abortion in America*, Boston, Massachusetts: Beacon Press, 1954, 1967.

BARBARA WASSERMAN, ed., *The Bold New Women*, New York: Fawcett, 1966.

"Selected Bibliography on Facilities for Early Childhood Care and Education," Ann Arbor, Michigan, Architectural Research Laboratory, University of Michigan, 1970.

Handbook on Women Workers, Women's Bureau Bulletin 294, U.S. Department of Labor, 1969.

"A Matter of Simple Justice," Report of the President's Task Force on Women's Rights and Responsibilities, Citizens' Advisory Council on the Status of Women, U.S. Department of Labor, 1970.

6

THE STRUGGLE
FOR JUSTICE:
Unfinished Revolution

CHANGING SEX ROLES IN THE
CONTEXT OF HISTORY

Social distinctions between men and women vary from generation to generation, as well as by social class and geographical region. For example, during the period preceding the agricultural and industrial revolution in the United States, women who migrated with their families from European countries worked at strenuous tasks that would both before and after this period have been considered wholly unfeminine. They produced large numbers of children and often died early, so it was not unusual for a man to have two or three families by the time he was old. But the work of pioneer women, however important and difficult, was always subsidiary. It was done with little or no remuneration, and was largely unskilled.

During the Victorian era, it was common for a middle-class or upper-class woman to feign illness in order to call attention to herself. It was also considered unbecoming for a lady to make herself useful or to show any signs of aggressiveness or humor. In such a situation, an aristocratic woman is said to have declared in all seriousness, "I have never met a man, however inferior, whom I do not consider to be my superior." [1]

Both pioneer wife and Victorian lady lacked political and economic power. They lacked the resources to choose their own destinies. But there is a difference in the way a woman views herself when she is a productive member of the society and when she is wholly dependent on others. When she undergoes a change from one perspective to another, the ideology or social myths that gave her support in one role must give way.

Because men have been able to view themselves as productive members of society more often, they have not needed as much ideological convincing to accept their positions. Rarely have they experienced drastic changes in their roles that demanded new ways of thinking about themselves. Whatever disadvantages may have been felt from time to time by men in their roles as men, they have not, at least in recent history, sought to change those roles through collective action, except in ameliorative ways. Women have led the way in creating ideological climates favorable to radical change.

But activity of this kind has been uneven. Periods marked by feminist activity seem to have occurred at those times when women's productive activity involved the sharing of a difficult job with men; specifically, when the job involved women and men in a struggle outside the home for other social changes considered important to both. The stage was then set for a woman to *recognize her disadvantaged position as a woman and for her to believe in the possibility and necessity of changing this position.*

Collective activity for women's rights can thus be seen as

1. Mrs. Humphry Ward, as quoted by Viola Klein, *The Feminine Character* (New York: International Universities Press, 1949), p. 24.

a response to complex historical conditions that gave women powers they had not experienced previously. At the same time, it brought their grievances into sharper focus.

Changes have not always produced greater freedom of choice for women. In some ways, women participated more freely in decision-making processes in ancient societies than they are able to do today—even with the vote and with greater control of childbearing. The following is an examination of the changes that did occur as a result of agitation for freedom.

THE AMERICAN EXPERIENCE

Records of American history show that women who participated in the Revolution against the Crown worked thereafter to win a place for themselves in local and state politics; their activity was followed by enactment of laws to prohibit such participation. During the Civil War, and before, when women abolitionists found themselves barred from international conferences on slavery and prohibited from speaking in public places, they organized to challenge the patriarchal order. Again, they were rebuffed even by their male colleagues, who reminded them that "this is the black man's hour." Their struggle continued, however. It was long and hard, and was renewed with vigor after the turn of the century, when men as well as women were caught up in the Age of Reform.

Each time, certain general social gains were made for women after changes in the productive relations of some men and women had been felt. First was recognition of women's *souls* by the church, which gave them a respect they had never known. Second was recognition of their *brains;* they were admitted to institutions of higher learning. Third, in recognition of their *political equality*, they gained the right to vote and to dissolve marital ties through divorce. After the 1920s, however, feminist activity waned, until the 1960s (again, following changes in economic relations and an era of political radicalism) when women again began asserting themselves collectively on their own behalf.

In every time period, there are a few women who challenge the stereotyped woman's role and who demand their "rights." There are a few who are able to express in writing the feelings of oppressed people everywhere. But only during times of social ferment have large numbers of men and women seen how inadequate the usual dominance-dependence relationships were for the conduct of a larger social struggle. Women *en masse* have then felt justified to move toward independence.

EFFECTS OF RELATED MOVEMENTS

The revolutionary struggles in the U.S.S.R., China, Algeria, Vietnam, and Cuba have all been accompanied by new, if in some cases short-lived, efforts to reconstruct sex roles. Less spectacular instances can be found in the histories of many other nations. Even the anti-British and, more recently, the anti-government activities of young people in contemporary Pakistan and India appear to have created a group of women leaders who are determined to improve the condition of women in these countries.

Accounts of these struggles are rarely found in the textbooks most commonly used in the United States. Few students can identify more than one or two feminist leaders even from their own national history. Few can describe the Seneca Falls Convention of 1848 and its historical setting, or relate the persecution and heroism of working women who organized to create tolerable conditions for themselves in the textile mills.

Not only is the feminist struggle given short shrift in the history books. The contributions of women leaders in other fields have also been given slight attention. Few students have any sense of the historical importance of work done by women for international peace, for establishing hospitals, for scientific research, for journalism, or for prison reform. Only the activities of women in the temperance movement, and the resulting sad experiment in prohibition, are recounted in most of the school materials read by students in the United States.

Women who are outstanding in their fields, including those who are given the recognition of Nobel Prizes, are seldom known to the general public. Only those women who gain fame through their association with famous men are voted Outstanding Woman of the Year by "average Americans."

THE POLITICAL HISTORY OF WOMEN
IN AMERICA

The history of American women is fascinating and complex. It cannot be related simply or in the space of a few pages. But it may be useful to provide here, in outline at least, a chronology of social action aimed at reconstructing the division of labor by sex.

Names included in this brief outline are representative figures who should not be construed as more important than other leaders whose names may have attracted less attention from historians, or whose contributions were made in more delimited spheres. Much study remains to be done to understand how and by whom changes in sex roles occurred.

Great Ladies of the Colonial and Revolutionary Periods

Outstanding among pre-revolutionary women was Anne Hutchinson, who insisted on her right to challenge theocratic doctrines and to speak publicly on religious matters. She was persecuted and subsequently banished from her Massachusetts community, but took with her a following of thirty-five families who settled in Providence, Rhode Island. Other early women leaders included Hannah Adams, who wrote numerous books on religious history, Abigail Adams, who published pamphlets urging revolutionary activity, Mercy Warren, whose personal correspondence with revolutionary leaders provided material for the first history of the American Revolution, and a number of widows such as Ann Franklin, who became prominent as managers of businesses and farms.

But neither these women, nor the many others who faced the harsh realities of the frontier, consciously organized other women to advance their common position in society. When larger numbers of women in colonial Massachusetts dared to rebel against restrictive roles, they were systematically persecuted and killed. When they collectively exercised the franchise in New Jersey, shortly after the end of the Revolutionary War, legislation was hurriedly enacted to prevent them from doing so again.

In the pre-industrial order, women who were slaves or bond servants working in the homes and fields of America were probably the most exploited members of the society, although many wives of pioneers fared little better.

Working Women of the Nineteenth Century

Diaries and letters of the women of the early nineteenth century reveal the developing ideal of the gentlewoman:

idle, delicate, pious, and finely dressed. But not everyone could afford to cultivate such gentility, and with the opportunity to leave the spinning wheel at home for work in the cotton mills, many women abandoned this dream forever. By the 1830s, women factory workers were organizing trade unions to increase wages and to improve the deplorable working conditions. A labor Reform Association was formed in 1845 to push for restrictions on working hours for women. Later working-class movements, such as the Grange movement, the Greenback Movement, and the Populist Movement, included many women and women leaders. A statement, pungent for its time, attributed to "the first powerful woman politician in the United States," Populist Mary Ellen Lease, advocated that "what the farmers need to do is raise less corn and more hell."

Development of Educational and Professional Opportunities

Girls' high schools were first established in the early 1800s, and a number of women's colleges were founded in the mid-1800s. The first institution of higher learning to enroll both men and women (and blacks) was Oberlin College, in 1833. Early efforts to educate former women slaves in the North were effectively squelched by hostile townspeople. Women who first entered professions such as medicine, law, and the ministry, and teachers of higher education were boycotted and shunned. Lucy Stone retained her maiden name upon marrying, and publicly repudiated the marriage laws at the time of her wedding. Of her efforts to speak in public, she said, "Yes, they threw eggs at me, but not *bad* eggs, as used to happen to earlier public speakers of my sex."

Discontent Spreads among Women of Leisure in the 1830s

Women's clubs and clandestine educational meetings pro-liferated in the 1830s, especially among businessmen's wives in the small towns of the Midwest. Women in various reform activities throughout the nation engaged in extended cor-respondence. They described the poverty of companionship that they found in marriage, and their yearning for friend-ship and common enterprise with others who were working for change. Among those who tirelessly studied, lectured, and organized against slavery and other social evils during this period was Lucretia Mott, a Quaker minister and teacher who continued her public work until her death in 1880.

Utopian Experiments of the Nineteenth Century

During the 1830s and 1840s, a number of communes and cooperatives in various parts of the country were established. The most well known were Brook Farm, the home of New England's literary elites, and the Oneida community in New York State. An industrial cooperative at Florence, Massachu-setts, included among its founders the ex-slave and heroine of abolition gatherings, Sojourner Truth.

In cooperative settlements, women worked alongside men in manual and productive tasks, and joined them in long hours of discussion and debate. Communalists dressed in comfortable clothing, ate simple foods, and, in some cases, shocked conventional morality by prohibiting marriage. The leader of one such community, socialist writer Robert Dale Owen, whose New Harmony Settlement in Indiana set the style for a number of other communal experiments, generated further hostility from his critics by authoring a birth con-trol guide entitled *Moral Physiology*.

Prelude to Seneca Falls

In 1840, a delegation of American abolitionists attended a World Anti-Slavery Conference in London. Women members were refused seats. They vowed to return to America and begin agitation for women's rights.

Eight years later, a convention was called at Seneca Falls, New York, to make a Declaration of Independence for women and to vote on a series of resolutions to guide the woman's rights movement. All resolutions passed unanimously, except the one concerning suffrage. At the second convention, held two years later, men took back seats and did not vote—a phenomenon that historians suggest had probably never occurred before anywhere in the world.

Here are excerpts from the 1848 Declaration:

> When, in the course of human events, it becomes necessary for one portion of the family of man to assume among the people of the earth a position different from that which they have hitherto occupied, but one to which the laws of nature and of nature's God entitle them, a decent respect to the opinions of mankind requires that they should declare the causes that impel them to such a course.
>
> We hold these truths to be self-evident: that all men and women are created equal; that they are endowed by their Creator with certain inalienable rights; that among these are life, liberty, and the pursuit of happiness; that to secure these rights governments are instituted, deriving their just powers from the consent of the governed. Whenever any form of government becomes destructive of these ends, it is the right of those who suffer from it to refuse allegiance to it, and to insist upon the institution of a new government, laying its foundation on such principles, and organizing its powers in such form, as to them shall seem most likely to effect their safety and happiness. Prudence, indeed, will

dictate that governments long established should not be changed for light and transient causes; and accordingly all experience hath shown that mankind are more disposed to suffer, while evils are sufferable, than to right themselves by abolishing the forms to which they were accustomed. But when a long train of abuses and usurpations, pursuing invariably the same object, evinces a design to reduce them under absolute despotism, it is their duty to throw off such government, and to provide new guards for their future security. Such has been the patient sufferance of the women under this government, and such is now the necessity which constrains them to demand the equal station to which they are entitled.

The history of mankind is a history of repeated injuries and usurpations on the part of man toward woman, having in direct object the establishment of an absolute tyranny over her. To prove this, let facts be submitted to a candid world.

He has never permitted her to exercise her inalienable right to the elective franchise.

He has compelled her to submit to laws, in the formation of which she had no voice.

He has withheld from her rights which are given to the most ignorant and degraded men . . . both natives and foreigners.

Having deprived her of this first right of a citizen, the elective franchise, thereby leaving her without representation in the halls of legislation, he has oppressed her on all sides.

He has made her, if married, in the eye of the law, civilly dead.

He has taken from her all right in property, even to the wages she earns.

He has made her, morally, an irresponsible being, as she can commit many crimes with impunity, provided they be done in the presence of her husband. In the covenant of marriage, she is compelled to promise obedience to her husband, he becoming, to all intents and purposes, her master . . . the law giving him power to deprive her of her liberty, and to administer chastisement.

He has so framed the laws of divorce, as to what shall be the proper causes, and in case of separation, to whom the guardianship of the children shall be given, as to be wholly regardless of the happiness of women . . . the law, in all cases, going upon the false supposition of the supremacy of man, and giving all power into his hands.

After depriving her of all rights as a married woman, if single, and the owner of property, he has taxed her to support a government which recognizes her only when her property can be made profitable to it.

He has monopolized nearly all the profitable employments, and from those she is permitted to follow, she receives but a scanty remuneration. He closes against her all the avenues to wealth and distinction which he considers most honorable to himself. As a teacher of theology, medicine, or law, she is not known.

He has denied her the facilities for obtaining a thorough education, all colleges being closed against her.

He allows her in Church, as well as State, but a subordinate position, claiming Apostolic authority for her exclusion from the ministry, and, with some exceptions, from any public participation in the affairs of the Church.

He has created a false public sentiment by giving to the world a different code of morals for men and women, by which moral delinquencies which exclude women from society, are not only tolerated, but deemed of little account in man.

He has usurped the prerogative of Jehovah himself, claiming as his right to assign for her a sphere of action, when that belongs to her conscience and to her God.

He has endeavored, in every way that he could, to destroy her confidence in her own powers, to lessen her self-respect, and to make her willing to lead a dependent and abject life.

Now, in view of this entire disfranchisement of one-half the people of this country, their social and religious degradation . . . in view of the unjust laws above mentioned, and because women do feel themselves aggrieved, oppressed, and fraudulently deprived of their most sacred rights, we insist that they have immediate admission to all the rights and privileges which belong to them as citizens of the United States.

In entering upon the great work before us, we anticipate no small amount of misconception, misrepresentation, and ridicule; but we shall use every instrumentality within our power to effect our object. We shall employ agents, circulate tracts, petition the State and National legislatures, and endeavor to enlist the pulpit and the press in our behalf. We hope this Convention will be followed by a series of Conventions embracing every part of the country.[2]

The Campaign to Reform Female Dress

The steel-ribbed and whaleboned corsets that kept women confined throughout the nineteenth century were briefly challenged at mid-century by Amelia Bloomer and others. They defiantly adopted comfortable apparel, only to succumb later to the scorn heaped upon them and their "bloomers." Many feminists of the nineteenth century regarded freedom of dress as important as economic opportunity and suffrage; but they were not united on strategic priorities.

Civil War Period

During the war, heroic women nurses emerged and subsequently established institutions for the training of women in nursing professions. Higher education for women ad-

2. This and other documents of the women's rights movement in the United States may be found in Aileen Kraditor, ed., *Up From the Pedestal* (Chicago: Quadrangle Books, 1968).

vanced rapidly after the war. Scientific doctrines such as Freudianism, Marxism, Darwinism, and theories regarding ancient matriarchies, provided new ideas about the natural qualities of womanness to be debated, and challenged the authority of scriptural doctrine in such matters. Feminist leaders who had worked hard on behalf of the emancipation of blacks felt betrayed when their own cause failed to gain support even from fellow abolitionists during and after the war. The Fourteenth and Fifteenth Amendments to the Constitution specified "male inhabitants" and "male citizens" in granting franchise to former slaves. This then legalized the disfranchisement of women and made necessary the long and difficult struggle to amend the federal Constitution in order to gain citizenship for women.

In 1867, an American Equal Rights Association was formed, advocating full citizen rights for blacks and women. Both issues lost during that year in a Kansas election.

The Movement Splits

A radical periodical, *The Revolution*, first published in 1868, focused on a feminist controversy centering around issues of militancy and radicalism. In 1869, the radical group, based in New York and led by Elizabeth Stanton and Susan Anthony, seceded from the Equal Rights Association. It formed an all-women National Women Suffrage Association. Soon after, Lucy Stone, Henry Ward Beecher, Julia Ward Howe, William Lloyd Garrison, and Theodore Higginson organized the American Women Suffrage Association, based in Boston. It published a new periodical, the *Woman's Journal*, as a mouthpiece for professional and middle-class suffragists. *The Revolution* did not survive the split and was abandoned in 1870. The two organizations vied for leadership of the suffrage movement until 1889, when they merged to form the National American Woman Suffrage Association.

Strains Focussed on the New Morality Issue

Victoria Woodhull, businesswoman and champion of "free love," withdrew from the National organization in 1872 to form a National Radical Reformers' Party. The party nominated her for President of the United States and nominated Frederick Douglass for Vice-President. In the periodical, *Woodhull and Chaflin's Weekly*, Miss Woodhull published an account of a scandalous love affair between suffragists, and was accused of seriously alienating the conservative public.

Literary Arguments Published

In 1883, a Victorian novel by Henry James, *The Bostonians*, berated the developing feminist ideology. His book foreshadowed a long period of literary attention to changing sex-role patterns, some supporting and some opposing the ideology of feminism. Similar European plays and novels, such as *A Doll's House* by Henrik Ibsen, were also widely read in the United States.

Women had begun to be active in the literary world earlier in the nineteenth century, but were generally engaged in writing journalistic pieces for "sentimental entertainment," which could be readily sold. In the Southern states, women writers published anonymously to protect their reputations. Such writing provided a new outlet for middle-class women, similar to the outlet factories provided for women who lived on farms and in city slums.

Lydia Maria Child, who wrote in the early 1800s a mild *Brief History of the Condition of Women in Various Ages and Nations,* later ruined her writing career when she published a series of fiery anti-slavery tracts.

States Grant Suffrage to Women

After extensive petitioning and organizing against heavy odds, the franchise for women was achieved, by the turn of the century, in four states: Wyoming, Utah, Colorado, and Idaho. Wyoming territory was the first to enfranchise women, in 1869. New Zealand was the first nation in the world to do so, in 1893.

> Altogether there were 480 campaigns to induce state legislatures to submit amendments to their electorates; 277 campaigns to persuade state party conventions to include women suffrage planks in their platforms . . . Between 1869 and 1916 there were 41 state amendment campaigns, with 9 victories and 32 defeats. Between the passage of the Utah and Idaho constitutional amendments in 1896 and the Washington victory in 1910 not one state enfranchised its women.[3]

Scholars attribute the early success of suffrage in frontier areas to a concern for establishing or preserving traditional Puritan morality. The revolutionary thinking of early suffragists was diluted by their need to gain majority approval from state legislators. The successful campaigns were those that also championed anti-immigration, anti-urban, and pro-racist causes. It is also likely, however, that women in frontier areas had achieved a measure of equality and respect through joining men in the battle for survival, which Eastern women, however well educated and vociferous, could not achieve.

3. Aileen Kraditor, *The Ideas of the Woman Suffrage Movement, 1890–1920* (New York: Columbia University Press, 1965), p. 5.

Marriage Laws Challenged

Divorce rates rose sharply between 1890 and 1900 and were attributed to the growth of feminist sentiment throughout the United States. A number of states introduced new legislation to cope with the problem. Restrictive legislation failed to pass in most cases, although the great debate over divorce that began in 1890 lasted for several decades.

Controversy over Religion Mounts in 1890s

A *Woman's Bible,* prepared by American suffragist Elizabeth Stanton and others, was published in Europe in 1895 to refute the doctrine of divine authorship of anti-feminist Biblical literature. While leaders such as Antoinette Brown attempted to reinterpret the Scriptures in support of feminist ideology, others, such as Ernestine Rose, declared that the movement did not need the support of Holy Writ. There was continual disagreement within the movement over the importance and validity of religious teachings. A number of leaders openly attacked organized religion, but others used organized religion as a public forum to advocate their cause. The first denominations to recognize women's claim to equality with men were Quakers, Unitarians, Universalists, and Shakers. More conservative groups responded to the feminist movement primarily by creating auxiliary orders to absorb women leaders. Enough women ministers existed, however, by 1882 to form their own national Woman's Ministerial Conference.

New Compromises Urged while Radical Wing Organizes Anew

A coalition of Southern, Western, and Eastern suffragists under the leadership of Anna Shaw, a medical doctor and minister, slowed the movement for radical social change and for concerted effort toward national suffrage legislation. They chose, instead, to try to get support for state legislation. At the same time, radical leaders, under the influence of English suffragettes and American intellectuals such as Charlotte Gilman, were forming a new political group and speaking out against the idolization of home and family.

Individuals of a more anarchistic persuasion championed women's rights in other ways. Emma Goldman, imprisoned for speaking in favor of birth control, also challenged on humanistic grounds the existence of the factory and of the nation-state.

Reformers of the Progressive Era Respond to Suffrage Movement

A general Federation of Women's Clubs numbered half a million members by 1914, among whom were members of the powerful Women's Christian Temperance Union. The Progressive Party, led by Theodore Roosevelt after his unsuccessful bid for the Republican nomination, gained the support of the Federation and, in return, supported woman suffrage. Cleavages then developed in the Progressive Movement over the issues of peace, prohibition, and economic legislation such as tariff regulation. Some of the leading suffragists worked actively for the Party.

Most well organized and well financed of the anti-suffrage forces was the liquor industry. Big political machines, too, were opposed until late in 1917. "Machine men were plainly uncertain of their ability to control an addition to the electorate which seemed to them relatively unsusceptible to bribery, more militant, and bent on disturbing reforms ranging from better sewage control to the abolition of child labor and, worst of all, 'cleaning up' politics." [4] Opponents of suffrage for women attempted to appeal especially to Catholic voters.

Working Women Push for Reform, Join Forces with Suffragists

Women of leisure and professional women joined with working women to form industrial leagues and settlement houses. Before the turn of the century, leaders of working women were cool toward the vote as a priority concern. Most came to support suffrage by the time the Socialist Party was at its height in the election of 1912. But controversy developed over the concern for improved working conditions, centering on the strategic importance of agitation for protective legislation versus agitation for equal rights legislation. Women organizers such as Mother Jones and Lenora O'Reilly were active in the American Federation of Labor, as earlier women had been in the Knights of Labor, and many suffered jail terms for their activities. Some, along with feminist Elizabeth Gurley Flynn, joined such revolutionary organizations as the International Workers of the World (IWW).

Attention Centers on Washington while Pressures on States Continue

A Congressional Union was organized by Alice Paul and Lucy Burns to re-focus attention on enactment of a constitutional amendment to secure the vote for women at the national level. In 1913, the CU merged with a militant organization, the Women's Political Union formed by Harriot

4. Eleanor Flexner, *Century of Struggle: The Woman's Rights Movement in the United States* (New York: Atheneum, 1968), p. 299.

Blatch in 1907 after the model of English organizations. Together they established a Woman's Party. The Party began
a series of dramatic lobbying, demonstrating, and picketing
efforts in Washington which, combined with the nationwide
educational activities of the more conservative but politically
revitalized National Association, under the leadership of
Carrie Catt, forced final passage of the Nineteenth Amendment late in 1919. Many of the militant women were jailed
for the pressures they exerted on President Wilson. He finally
promised support of suffrage in order to prevent anti-war
groups from borrowing the women's tactics or joining the
ranks of suffragists. His support eventually secured the one
vote in the Senate that had been lacking for over a year.

1920–1960

One author depicts this period as the age of The New
Victorians. Such social changes as occurred in other industrialized countries along with or following the enfran-
chisement of women failed to occur in the United States. For
instance, in Germany, married feminists gave up the title
"Frau" and identified themselves along with their unmarried
sisters as "Fraulein." In the Scandinavian countries, state insurance was provided for maternity and three years of child
care, the latter given optionally to men or women. The rights
of illegitimate children were protected (most thoroughly in
Norway). And increasingly, women demanded economic
changes that would make it possible for women to "love
work, love love, and love children all at the same time." [5]
No such major changes occurred in the United States, although professional women organized to advance their own

5. Katherine Anthony, *Feminism in Germany and Scandinavia* (New
York: Henry Holt and Co., 1915), p. 204.

positions, and individual men and women continued to write and to research the position of women in society.

During World War II, many women experienced the kind of independence that comes from working for pay with other men and women, at jobs deemed necessary and demanding. It is possible that their experiences contributed—if only through a delayed reaction—to the revival of feminist activity a decade later.

In the meantime, a generation of women who came to maturity in the 1950s were exposed to a carefully cultivated "feminine mystique," which, combined with restricted opportunities for work, kept many of them at least temporarily in domestic and subsidiary roles.

1960–1970

Revival of debate and action around the issue of feminism followed close on the heels of the formation of the National Organization for Women (NOW), the passage of Civil Rights legislation, and the appointment of a National Commission on the Status of Women, all in 1963–64. More radical groups emerged from anti-war and Black Power activity during the mid-sixties. A black woman had initiated activity for social justice by refusing to move to the back seat of a Jim Crow bus. In the struggles that followed, women discovered their own degradation and exploitation when they attempted to work in partnership with men. By 1969, there were women's caucuses and resolutions on "women's liberation" in most "Movement" organizations. Local Women's Liberation chapters or groups of Radical Women formed on every major university and college campus in America. Experimental communes grew up across the nation to explore alternative life styles for men and women. In 1968, a "Coalition of the Young, the Black, and the Beautiful" seceded from NOW and began an anti-Establishment action group. The same year the first National Conference of Radical Women met in Chicago. In the fall of 1969, *Women: a journal of liberation* began publication to complement local publication efforts of the rapidly growing Women's Liberation Movement. By the end of 1970, not only were women's rights activities featured regularly in the Establishment press, but reprints of historical documents were also made widely available,[6] and at least a dozen feminist journals, literary magazines, and nationally circulated newspapers were published regularly.[7]

6. *Source Library of the Women's Movement*, 40 titles, 63 volumes (New York: Source Book Press, 1970); *Women's Rights and Liberation: Out-of-print Books and Pamphlets* (Chatham, New Jersey: The Chatham Bookseller).

7. *Tooth and Nail*, c/o Wesley Foundation, 2398 Bancroft Way, Berkeley, California 94704; *Off the Pedestal*, 376 Addison Street, Palo Alto, California 94301; *Off Our Backs*, 2318 Ashmead Place NW (basement), Washington, D.C. 20009; *Socialist Woman*, 21 Watcombe Circus, Carrington, Nottingham, England; *Women's Monthly*, c/o Media Women, Box 1592, New York, New York 10001; *Bread and Roses Newsletter*, Box 116, Cambridge, Massachusetts 02138; *It Ain't Me Babe*, c/o WL Office, 2398 Bancroft Avenue, Berkeley, California 94704; *Rat*, 241 E. 14th Street, New York, New York 10003; *Up From Under*, 339 Lafayette Street, New York, New York 10012; *No More Fun and Games*, A Journal for Female Liberation, c/o Female Liberation, 371 Somerville Avenue, Somerville, Massachusetts 02143; *Women Speak Out*, 1376 Hollister Road, Cleveland Heights, Ohio 44118; *Voice of Women's Liberation*, 1545 Claremont, Chicago, Illinois 60622; *Women*, 225 Park Avenue, Room 333, New York, New York 10017; *Connections* (Prison Widows), c/o C. Kornblith, 70 Liberty Street, San Francisco, California 94110; *New York Feminist*, 2000 Broadway, New York, New York 10023; *Pedestal*, c/o Vancouver Women's Liberation, 307 W. Broadway, Vancouver, British Columbia, Canada; *Women: A Journal of Liberation*, 30011 Guilford Avenue, Baltimore, Maryland 21218; *Aphra*, Box 355, Springtown, Pennsylvania 18081; *Up From Radicalism: A Feminist Journal*, c/o Bantam Books, 666 5th Avenue, New York, New York 10019; *A Feminist Journal*, 483 West Lynnhurst #25, St. Paul, Minnesota 55104; *Lilith*, c/o Women's Majority Union, Box 1895, Seattle, Washington 98111; *Everywoman*, 6516 W. 83rd Street, Los Angeles, California 90045; *Red Star: Organ of Red Women's Detachment*, 700 E. 9th Street, New York,

These publications show increasing concern with the limitations imposed on children and on women and men by the nuclear family, by monogamy, and by the society's emphasis on heterosexual relations. They emphasize increasingly "sisterhood" among women of all social classes and races and point out the necessity for men to form their own "men's liberation" groups as an appropriate response to the Women's Liberation Movement. Their pages also present a developing radical interpretation of the problem of sexism. They see the current social emphases on privatism and consumerism, the continued insistence on *caste* divisions in the office, school, and factory as supporting economic institutions that are inherently chauvinistic and dehumanizing. Contemporary feminists say that it is necessary to transform the economic base of American society in order to bring it under the control of producers and consumers who are more likely to be concerned about human needs than about corporate expansion.

OLD PROBLEMS AND NEW POSSIBILITIES

Facets of struggle in the movement today include the seeking of new constituencies in the suburbs, ghettoes, and factories through activity in unions, churches, schools, and businesses; conducting workshops and teach-ins; holding retreats (called "non-retreats" or "survival revivals"); establishing new talk, study, and action groups; encouraging women's caucuses in political and professional organizations; planning demonstrations; researching, writing, and publish-

New York 10009; *Southern Journal of Female Liberation,* c/o Southern Female Rights Union, Box 30087, Lafayette Square Station, New Orleans, Louisiana 70130; *Current Women's Liberation Material Newsletter,* c/o Laure X, 2325 Oak Street, Berkeley, California 94708; *Pandora's Box,* Box 22094, San Diego, California 92122.

ing. Women who have been involved in the Women's Liberation Movement over a period of years are forming living collectives (some for both men and women and some for women only) to further their work potential and to provide the support and strength they need to survive in a manipulative, repressive, and sometimes hostile environment.

Historical materials related to the Women's Rights Movement describe the issues, public fears, and responses that are still encountered by feminists today. Contemporary feminists realize that change is not always rapid or steady, and that it does not always occur for the reasons or with the consequences one might wish. They view today's tasks in their uniqueness as well as in their relation to the past, building as they must on previous successes and failures.

It is true that other societies, in which efforts toward egalitarianism have been made, have sometimes retrogressed to less-than-revolutionary policies, as in the U.S.S.R. during the period when Stalin destroyed the Soviets and consolidated state power, and in the nations of Eastern Europe where party rule became absolute. Some day care centers have been closed down in Yugoslavia; abortions have been made more difficult in Rumania; women have resumed kitchen work in the Israeli kibbutzim; Russian women have been encouraged to retreat to home and family. The major reason given for such retrogressive measures has been, interestingly, the decline of birth rates.[8]

8. See the following sources for discussions of the struggle against sexism in other countries:

Simone de Beauvoir, *The Long March* (New York: World Publishing Co., 1958); Jack Belden, "Sex and Revolution," *Monthly Review*, 22, 4 (1970): 47–57; Margaret Benston, "The Political Economy of Women's Liberation," *Monthly Review*, September, 1969;

Donald R. Brown, ed., *The Role and Status of Women in the Soviet Union* (New York: Teacher's College Press, Columbia University, 1968); Kamila Chulinska, "Political Activity of Women in Eastern Europe," *The*

The proponents of women's liberation in America today are convinced that such problems are now amenable to solution, perhaps for the first time in history. Collective modes of production have been so highly developed that scarcities of labor and goods exist only because of social or psychological reasons and not because of material or technological ones. Americans consume and destroy an inordinate amount of the world's material resources. As such inequities are challenged, people can work together, not for survival alone, but

Annals of the American Academy of Political and Social Science, 375 (January, 1968): 67–71;

Marcelle Devaud, "Political Participation of Western European Women," *The Annals of the American Academy of Political and Social Science,* 375 (January, 1968): 61–66;

Felix Greene, *Awakened China: The Country Americans Don't Know,* Garden City (New York: Doubleday and Co., 1961);

Fanina W. Halle, *Women in Soviet Russia* (New York: Viking Press, 1935);

William Hinton, *Fanshen, A Documentary of Revolution in a Chinese Village* (New York: Random House, 1968);

Linda Jenness, Fidel Castro, *Women and the Cuban Revolution* (New York: Pathfinder Press, 1970);

Laurie Landy, *Women in the Chinese Revolution* (New York: International Socialist Book Service, 1970);

Birgitta Liner, Richard Litell, *Sex and Society in Sweden* (New York: Random House, 1967);

The Status of Women in Sweden, Swedish Information Service, Stockholm, 1967;

Vera Mace and David Mace, *The Soviet Family* (Garden City, New York: Doubleday and Co., 1963);

Karl Marx, Nicolai Lenin, Frederick Engels, Joseph Stalin, *The Woman Question: Selections* (New York: International Publishers, 1969);

Jan Myrdal, *Report from a Chinese Village* (New York: Random House, 1965);

Juliet Mitchell, "Women: The Longest Revolution," *New Left Review,* 40 (November/December, 1968);

Peter B. Neubauer, ed., *Children in Collectives; Child-Rearing Aims and Practices in the Kibbutz* (Springfield, Illinois: Charles C. Thomas Publications, 1965);

Helen Foster Snow, *Women in Modern China* (Paris: Mouton & Co., 1967);

Jose Yglesias, *In the Fist of the Revolution* (New York: Random House, 1969);

"Women in Revolution," special issue of *Women: A Journal of Liberation,* Summer, 1970, Baltimore, Maryland.

also for the development of their human potential. And women, with men as part of humankind, will be free to pursue the yet-to-be-realized ideal, "from each according to her (or his) ability; to each according to her (or his) needs." [9]

REFERENCES

MARY BEARD, *On Understanding Women*, New York: Longmans, Green & Co., 1931.

CHARLOTTE PERKINS GILMAN, *Women and Economics*, New York: Harper & Row, Publishers, 1966 (originally published in 1898).

WILLIAM GOODE, *World Revolution and Family Patterns*, New York: The Free Press, 1963, 1968.

ALAN B. GRIMES, *The Puritan Ethic and Woman Suffrage*, New York: Oxford University Press, Inc., 1967.

INEZ HAYNES IRWIN, *Angels and Amazons*, Garden City, New York: Doubleday & Company, Inc., 1933.

INEZ HAYNES IRWIN, *The Story of the Woman's Party*, New York: Harcourt Brace Jovanovich, Inc., 1921.

WILLIAM O'NEILL, *Everyone Was Brave: The Rise and Fall of Feminism in America*, Chicago: Quadrangle Books, 1969.

ANDREW SINCLAIR, *The Better Half: The Emancipation of the American Woman*, New York: Harper & Row, Publishers, 1965.

MARY WHITTON, *These Were the Women: U.S.A. 1776–1860*, New York: Hastings House, 1954.

9. See the following source for my own analysis of the relationship between sexism and capitalism. Carol Andreas, "Notes on the Liberation of Women," *Sociology in the Seventies: An Activist Perspective* (New York: John Wiley and Sons, 1971).

INDEX